MES

OF

THE QUEEN OF PEACE

1981-2014

"Dear Children! In a special way, today I am calling you to prayer. Pray, little children, so that you may comprehend who you are and where you need to go. Be carriers of the good news and be people of good hope. Be love for all those who are without love. Little children, you will be everything and will achieve everything only if you pray and are open to God's will – to God who desires to lead you to eternal life. I am with you and intercede for you from day to day before my Son Jesus. Thank you for having responded to my call." 25-11-2014

JOE AND ELEANOR MCFADDEN
DUBLIN, IRELAND
Email: medjugorje.messages@outlook.com
Ph. + 353 1 4979186
DECEMBER 2014

Dedication
FOR THE INTENTIONS
of Our Lady Queen of Peace

Permission

Permission to print this book has been received from
Information Centre "Mir" Medjugorje
which also provided the translation from Croatian to English
Gospin trg 1, 88266 Medjugorje, Bosnia i Herzegovina
Website: http//www.medjugorje.ie

Photographs

McFadden Records
Vicka and Marija in Ireland (David Parkes - Marian
Pilgrimages), Ivan in Ireland (Philip Ryan, Joe Walsh
Tours, Finbar O'Leary), Photo Đani - Medjugorje

Printers

Grafotisak, Grude
www.grafotisak.com

Authority

The publishers recognise and accept that the final
authority regarding the validity of claimed apparitions
rests with the Catholic Church and the Holy See of
Rome, and willingly await and submit to the final
results of the ongoing investigations into the events in
Medjugorje.

Publishers

Joe and Eleanor McFadden
Email: medjugorje.messages@outlook.com
December 2014
Ph. +353 1 497 9186

ISBN No: 978-0-9562317-5-8

TABLE OF CONTENTS

Marija Pavlovic-Lunetti in Dublin 21-2-2013 4

Greetings from Viska Ivankovic-Mijatovic 5

Background to Introduction by Fr. Slavko O.F.M. 6

Introduction by Fr. Slavko O.F.M. 8

Sequence of the Messages by Fr. Ljudevit Rupic O.F.M 13

    The First Seven Days 13

    Five Themes of Our Lady's Messages 21

    Special Messages to the Parish and Pilgrims 26

    Weekly Messages (1984-1987) 28

    Monthly Messages (1987-2013) 72

Diagram illustrating the Five Themes and Messages 210

The importance of the Messages 221

The Purpose and Mysteries of the Holy Rosary 224

The Recitation of the Holy Rosary 226

The Sacrament of Penance and Reconciliation 227

The Way of the Cross 229

Holy Places for Reflection 230

Map of Medjugorje area 231

Basic tips for travelling 232

Where to obtain this book 233

Publisher's Note 234

As of today, may new life begin in your heart. Children, I desire to see your "yes", and may your life be a joyful living of God's will at every moment of your life. ..." (25-3-2011)

Marija pictured during her apparition in Dublin on Thursday February 21st 2013

Vicka Ivanković-Mijatović greets readers of this series

Dragi prijatelji!

Puno vas pozdravlja
i mali za sve vas
vaša Vicka

Translation

Dear Friends,
I'm sending my regards and I am praying for all of you.

Yours Vicka

Given on 29th October 2008 in person.

Vicka awaits Our Lady, Dublin February 2011

Background to "Introduction by Fr. Slavko Barbaric O.F.M."

When working with Fr. Slavko over 16 years, I would often arrive in Medjugorje with pilgrims, and request some help from him, regarding spreading the Messages. He spoke in 18 venues in Ireland and we were well used to working with him. He would always say "yes" to the request, and then ask when the "dead line" would be. I always thought he would forget ,he was so extraordinarily busy, but 48 hours before going home he would always have the work requested done.

On the Feast of the Assumption, 15th August 1986, forty eight hours before I left Medjugorje, I spotted Fr. Slavko going up the steps of the Presbytery at 10pm. He had unusually long days, climbing Krizevac (1600 ft.) every morning, before 7.30a.m. Holy Mass. That day he had then hosted thousands of pilgrims, leading them in prayer throughout the day. He must have been exhausted. Nevertheless, I took the courage to run over to the steps and enquired had he managed to do the preface for our book of Messages which I had requested on arrival. He was at the top of the steps. " I will do it right now", he answered, I said "I don't mean right now, you must be exhausted?" He ran down the steps and came over to me and said," but what about you, are you not also exhausted?" That was Fr. Slavko. He was always thinking of others.

Fr. Slavko was well known to take just a few hours sleep at night. He worked for Our Lady tirelessly and selflessly. That night he wrote the following text, and gave it to me the next day. Typical Fr. Slavko!!

Eleanor McFadden

Introduction

Fr. Slavko Barbaric O.F.M. (1946-2000)

Dear Readers,

We are now in the sixty – second month since the Apparitions began and I am sure that many of you have already read a lot about the Apparitions in the last months. We would like to offer you this new book and with this new book we would to give you new impulses. The Apparitions have now lasted, when you count in days, one thousand eight hundred and sixty days. That means, so many times Our Lady invited us to Peace, to Prayer, to Fasting, to Conversion and to Faith and it could easy happen that over here we do not listen to this message any more. Subconsciously we could develop the reaction – Oh! I know about that already. But this is not what it is all about whether we know it or don't know it. In the Apparitions in any case there are no new contents. Everything comes from the Gospel. It is important for us to get a new impulse, a new move and that is why I would like to address this text to everybody, to all people who know about the Apparitions from the start.

The Mother of God does not want us to get tired. She wants us to get deeper into Faith, the longer we know about these Apparitions and Messages, and with us exactly the opposite can happen. The longer we know about it, the less we are interested and the less we are moved. You want Messages she said – and I am tired. That means she will not leave us alone, she will not leave us in peace, so to speak, as long as we have not found what she is educating us for.

I would like to say a word to all those who only come to the cross through these Messages. Many have heard about the Messages through books for the first time and all those and all those who have started to do what Our Lady says – they have gone ahead. Their interest in the Messages has grown, and through the interest, peace has grown. I would like everybody who gets in touch with the Messages for the first time to experience joy, and I would like them to experience the presence of Our Lady, even if just through a book. And so that is why I am speaking to everybody. Those who have known about it before and want to get on, and also those who have got started and have become stuck half way through tiredness or whatever, and I would like to speak to those also who get in touch for the first time.

For all of us the Messages have the same meaning. Again we are all invited now. The excuses we use – I didn't know about it before or I knew about it already – they shouldn't be valid now. We are all called to the same thing – be reconciled. We are all concerned in the same way to the call of Peace and the same thing is for us – we are all called to Prayer and Fasting in the same way. Have I transmitted to you the five main points that Our Lady is concerned about. She calls us to Peace. She did not say I have come to tell you that you need Peace. We know that we need Peace even without Apparitions, but She has come to show us the way to find that Peace. She showed us the way to Peace. She said "convert". That means change your life, change your behaviour and that means change everything in the light of the love for God and the fellowman and don't be tired in those changes. She calls us to use the means She gives us to live that change and those are prayer, fasting and faith. Through fasting and prayer she wants to bring God into our lives, and there where God is present, peace Exists, and there where God comes life exists. We are longing for the peace in life and love. Why should we not all hear about that again? We are all longing for it and She touches the deepest longing that we have within ourselves. She asks us to open our hearts so that God can come into them, so that He can give us what really desire. Those five main Messages are like directives on our way.

Since the 1st March, 1984, Our Lady has started to give what are called the Thursday Messages. The more we meet those Messages and are living with them, the more we talk about them, the more we think about them, the more we see that every single Message, even if it is very simple, is important. These Messages are like a weekly invitation to the first Messages, and the Thursday Messages are to keep us awake. If we get tired, they give us new strength. Or if we ask "what exactly am I to do now" we get an answer.

If I should make a résumé of what She says in the Thursday Messages, She always repeats – Pray, Pray, Pray; then She always says why? Pray that you shall find peace. Pray and then you will be able to love, and through love, you will overcome sin and difficulties. Pray and your faith will grow. Pray and you will grow in holiness. Very often She spoke of our duties. She said once to help the others who do not yet know how to live in a holy manner and in a holy way. Carry faith to the world that is living in darkness. Bring light, unity and peace to the others. This is what She expects from us.

It is normal that after five years that She never invited us to criticise. There are enough people in the world who criticise and judge. We do not have enough of those who carry the light and peace. We Christians should be the first ones in that duty and really the ones who are never tired. From whom should this world expect something if not from us Christians? Or what do we want the world to be redeemed with, and that it is only in the second place that we should carry love and peace as Christians. Jesus did not think and act in this way, and Mary wants us to learn the way of behaving like Jesus did. This is certainly not an easy way, because we are very often too hard, because very often we are deep in sin and we need a very long purification process. Our Lady is very patient with us and we should be patient with each other and I would like us all to remain that way. I would like to end this introduction with the words She always says "Thank you for responding to my call" because if you have responded, you have peace.

Medjugorje, 15th August, 1986
The Feast of the Assumption of Our Lady

"…I rejoice with you and I desire to tell you that your brother Slavko has been born into Heaven and intercedes for you…" (25-11-2000)

The Sequence of the Messages

Fr. Ljudevit Rupčić O.F.M. (1920-2003)

The First Seven Days (24-30 June 1981)

The first day

On the said date at approximately six o' clock in the evening, on the area of Crnica hill known as Podbrdo, the children, Ivanka Ivanković, Mirjana Dragićević, Vicka Ivanković, Ivan Dragićević, Ivan Ivanković and Milka Pavlović saw an incredibly beautiful young woman with a little child in her arms. She didn't say anything to them but indicated with gestures that they should come closer. Surprised and frightened they were afraid to come near, even though they immediately thought her to be Our Lady.

The second day

On the second day, the 25th of June 1981, the children agreed to meet once again at the same place that Our Lady had previously appeared, in the hope of seeing her again. All of a sudden there was a flash of light. The children looked up and saw Our Lady, this time without the Child. She was smiling and joyful and was indescribably beautiful. With her hands she gestured to them to come closer. The children braced themselves and went up to her. They immediately fell to their knees and began to pray the "Our Father, Hail Mary and Glory Be". Our Lady prayed together with them except for when they prayed the "Hail Mary".

After the prayer she began to speak with the children. Ivanka, first of all, asked about her mother who had died two months previously. Mirjana asked Our Lady for some sign to be given to show to the people that they were neither lying nor crazy, as some people had said.

Our Lady finally left the children with the words, "God be with you my angels!" Before that, when the children asked her if they would see her the following day, she replied by nodding her head.

According to the visionaries the whole encounter was indescribable. On that day two of the children, which made up the previous group were missing: Ivan Ivanković and Milka Pavlović. They were replaced by two others: Marija Pavlović and Jakov Čolo. And from that day onwards according to these six children, Our Lady regularly appears to them. Milka Pavlović and Ivan Ivanković, who were present on the first day of apparitions, did not see Our Lady again, even though they returned to the apparition site, in the hope of seeing her.

The third day

On the 26th of June 1981, the children full of anticipation waited at around six o' clock, which was when she previously appeared. They were going towards the same place, to meet her there. They were very happy, although their joy was mixed with fear wondering what would be the outcome of all this. Despite all this, the children could feel some sort of inner strength attracting them to meet with Our Lady.

Suddenly, while the children were still on their way a light flashed three times. To them and to those following them, it was a sign indicating Our Lady's whereabouts. On that third day Our Lady appeared even higher up than on the previous days. All at once Our Lady disappeared. But when the children began to pray, she reappeared. She was cheerful and smiling serenely and once again her beauty was overwhelming.

As they left their houses some older women advised them to carry holy water with them to make sure that the vision was not of Satan. When they were with Our Lady Vicka took the water and splashed it in the direction of the vision saying, "If you are Our Blessed Mother, please stay, and if you are not, go away from us". Our Lady smiled at this and remained with the children. Then Mirjana asked her name and she replied, "I am the Blessed Virgin Mary".

On the same day, coming down Podbrdo, Our Lady appeared one more time, this time however only to Marija saying, "Peace, peace, peace and only peace". Behind her, Marija could see a cross. After which Our Lady repeated, in tears, the following words, "Peace must reign between man and God, and between all people!" The area where this took place is about half way up to the Apparition Site.

The fourth day

On the 27th of June 1981, Our Lady appeared three times to the children. On that occasion the children asked all kinds of questions and Our Lady responded. For priests, she gave this message. "May the priests firmly believe and may they take care of the faith of the people!" Once again, Jakov and Mirjana asked for a sign, because the people had begun to accuse them of lying and of taking drugs. "Do not be afraid of anything", Our Lady replied.

Before parting, when asked if she would come again, she indicated that she would. On the way down Podbrdo, Our Lady appeared one more time to say goodbye with the words, "May God be with you my angels, go in peace!"

The fifth day

On the 28th of June 1981, big crowds were gathering from all parts even from the early hours of the morning. By noon there were about fifteen thousand people. On the same day, the Parish Priest, Fr. Jozo Zovko, examined the children on what they had seen and heard in the previous days.

At the usual time Our Lady appeared again. The children prayed with her, and afterwards they questioned her. Vicka, for example, asked "My dear Lady, what do you want from us and what do you want from our priests?" Our Lady replied, "The people should pray and firmly believe". Regarding priests, she replied that they should believe firmly and help others to do the same.

On that day Our Lady came and went many times. During one of these times the children asked her why she doesn't appear in the Parish Church for every one to see. She replied, "Blessed are those who have not seen and yet believe".

Even though the crowds were pushing them with their questions and curiosities and the day was heavy and sultry, the children felt as though they were in heaven.

The sixth day

On the 29th of June 1981, the children were taken to Mostar for a medical examination after which they were proclaimed "healthy". The statement of the head doctor was: "The children aren't crazy, the person who brought them here must be though"....

The crowds on Apparition Hill that day were greater than ever. As soon as the children arrived at the usual place and began to pray, Our Lady appeared. On that occasion the Blessed Mother exhorted them to have faith saying, "The people should believe firmly and have no fear."

On that day, a doctor who was following and observing them, during the apparition desired to touch Our Lady. The children guided her hand to the place where Our Lady's shoulder was, and she felt a tingling sensation. The doctor, even though an atheist had to admit that, "Here, something strange is happening!".

On that same day a child was miraculously healed by the name of Daniel Šetka whose parents had come to Medjugorje, praying specifically for a healing. Our Lady had promised that this would come about if the parents prayed and fasted and strongly believed. The child thereupon was healed.

The seventh day

On the 30th of June 1981 two young girls suggested to the children to go by car further away to be able to stroll in peace. Really their intention was to bring them away from the area and keep them until after the normal apparition time had passed. However, even though the children were far away from Podbrdo, at the usual time of the apparition, it was as if an interior call prompted them to ask to be let out of the car. As soon as they did, and said a prayer, Our Lady drew near to them, from the direction of Podbrdo, which was now over a kilometre away. She prayed seven "Our Father's, Hail Mary's and Glory be to the Father's". So the girls' trick had no effect. Soon after this the police began to hinder the children and the pilgrims going on Podbrdo, the site of apparitions. The children, and soon afterwards even the crowds were forbidden to go there. But Our Lady continued to appear to them in secret places, in their homes and in the fields. The children had already gained confidence, and openly spoke with Our Lady, eagerly seeking her advice, listening to her warnings and messages. The events of Medjugorje continued in this fashion up until the 15th of January 1982.

In the meantime, the Parish Priest began to host the pilgrims in the Church, enabling them to participate in the rosary and to celebrate the

Eucharist. The children also gave out the rosary. Our Lady sometimes appeared to them in the church at that time. Even the Parish Priest himself once while praying the rosary, saw Our Lady. Immediately he broke off praying and spontaneously started to sing a popular hymn: "Lijepa si, lijepa, Djevo Marijo" - "O how beautiful you are, Most Blessed Virgin Mary". The whole church could see that something unusual was happening to him. Afterwards he stated that he had seen her. And so, he who up until then had not only been doubtful, but openly against even rumours of the apparitions, became their defender. He testified his support of the apparitions even to the point of serving a prison sentence.

From the 15th of January 1982 onwards the children saw Our Lady in a closed off area of the Parish Church. The Parish Priest arranged this because of the newly arisen difficulties and sometimes even dangers, which provided themselves for the visionaries. Previously the children had ensured that this was in accord with Our Lady's wishes. Because of the prohibitions of the Diocesan Bishop however, from April 1985 onwards the children ceased to use the area of the church as an apparition site. Instead, they went to a room in the Parish house.

All this time, from the beginning of the apparitions up until today, there have only been five days when none of the children saw Our Lady.

Our Lady didn't always appear in the same place either, nor to the same group, nor individuals, nor did her apparitions always last a specified period. Sometimes the apparitions lasted two minutes, sometimes an hour. Neither did Our Lady appear at the children's will. Sometimes they prayed and waited but Our Lady didn't appear until a little while afterwards, unexpectedly and unforewarned. And sometimes she appeared to one and not to the others. If she hadn't promised an appointed time, nobody knew when she would appear, or if she would appear. Neither did she appear always to just the aforesaid visionaries, but to others also of different age, stature, race, education and walks of life. All this suggests that the apparitions are not a product of the imagination. It depends neither on time nor place, nor desire nor the prayer of pilgrim or visionary, but moreover on the will of He who permits it.

Five Themes of Our Lady's Messages

According to the united testimony of the visionaries, Our Lady during her apparitions gives a series of messages, to be transmitted to the people. Even though there are many messages, they can however be summarized in five themes, because all the messages basically underline or lead up to these five.

Peace

Already on the third day, Our Lady stressed peace as the first of her messages: "Peace, peace, peace and only peace!", after which she said twice, "Peace must reign between God and man and between people". Considering that Marija could see a cross, when Our Lady gave this message, the obvious conclusion is that this peace comes from God. God, who through Our Lady in Christ became our peace.(Ephesians 2:14)"For He is the peace between us"...This peace, "the world cannot give"(John 14:27)and that's why Christ commanded His apostles to bring it to the world (Matthew 10:11) so that all men could become "sons of peace"(Luke 10:6). That's why Our Lady as "Queen of Apostles" in Medjugorje specifically refers to herself as "Queen of Peace". Who better than she can more successfully convince today's world, which is faced with the threat of destruction, how great and necessary peace is.

Faith

The second of Our Lady's messages is faith. Already on the fourth, fifth and sixth day of apparitions, Our Lady exhorted those present to have strong faith. Understandably, she repeated this message many times. Without faith we cannot arrive at peace! Not only this but faith is itself an answer to God's Word, which He not only proclaims but actually gives to us. When we believe, we accept God's Word, which in Christ became "our peace"(Ephesians 2:14). Accepting it, the individual becomes a new creature, with a new life of Christ within, and a share in God's nature (1 Peter 1:4, Ephesians 2:18) In this way the individual ensures peace with God and with others.

Once again there is no one who can better understand the necessity and efficaciousness of faith than Our Lady. That's why she stressed it on every occasion and charged the visionaries to bring the light of faith to others. Our Lady presented faith as an answer to everything, no matter whatever people were looking for. She presented it as the pre-requisite of all prayer, desires and demands, relating it to health, wholeness and to all other human necessities.

Conversion

Conversion was another one of Our Lady's frequent messages. This presupposes that she noticed either a weakness or a complete lack of faith in humanity today. And without conversion it is impossible to achieve peace. True conversion means, the purifying or cleansing of the heart (Jeremiah 4:14), because a corrupt or 'deteriorated' heart is the basis of bad relations, which in turn brings social disorder, unjust laws, base constitutions etc. Without a radical change of heart, without the conversion of the heart, there is no peace. For this reason, Our Lady continually suggests frequent confession. The request is directed to all without differentiation because, "not one of us is just"...."all have wandered, not one does right"(Romans 3:11-12).

Prayer

Almost daily, from the fifth day of apparitions onwards Our Lady recommends prayer. She requests everyone to "pray without ceasing" just as Christ himself taught (Mark 9:29, Matthew 9:38; Luke 11:5-13). Prayer, therefore stimulates and strengthens our faith, without which our relationship with God is disordered, as is our relationship with each other. Prayer also reminds us of how close God is to us even in our daily lives. In prayer we acknowledge Him, we give Him thanks for His gifts to us, and we are filled with a hopeful expectancy of that which we need, but particularly our redemption. Prayer solidifies the equilibrium of the individual, and aids us in our 'ordered relationship with God', without which it is impossible to maintain peace either with God or with our neighbour.

The Word of the Lord acquainted itself with all humanity and awaits humanity's response. It is precisely this which gives prayer it's "justification". Our response should be "spoken faith", or "prayer". In prayer, faith animates, renews, strengthens and sustains itself. In addition to this, man's prayer really bears witness to the Gospel, and to the existence of God, thus provoking a response of faith in others.

Fasting

Already on the sixth day of the apparitions, Our Lady often recommended fasting because it aids faith. That is, the practice of fasting aids and ensures control over oneself. Only the person who can dominate himself is truly free, and is capable of abandoning himself to God and to his neighbour, as faith demands. Fasting guarantees him that his abandonment to faith is secure and sincere. It helps him to free himself from every slavery, but especially to the slavery of sin. Whoever is not in the possession of oneself is in some way enslaved. Therefore fasting helps the individual to restrain himself from disordered pleasure seeking which in turn leads him to a futile and useless existence often wasteful of the very goods which are necessary to others just for basic survival.

With fasting we also receive the gift, which creates within us a realistic love for the poor and the destitute, which up to a certain point eases the difference between rich and poor. It therefore heals the wants of the poor and also heals the excesses and over-indulgence of others. And in it's own way, it gives a dimension of peace which today in a special way, is threatened by the difference in the lifestyles of the rich and the poor. (e.g. North and South).

To sum up, we can say that Our Lady's Messages underline that peace is the greatest good, and that faith, conversion, prayer and fasting are the means by which we can attain it.

Special Messages to the Parish and Pilgrims

Outside of the five messages which, as we have said are the important messages which Our Lady immediately gave to the whole world, she started from the 1st of March 1984, every Thursday, mainly through the visionary Marija Pavlović to give special messages to the Parish of Medjugorje and to the pilgrims who come. Our Lady therefore, outside of the six visionaries chose the Parish of Medjugorje together with the pilgrims who come here to be her collaborators and witnesses. This is clear from the first of the Thursday messages, where she says: "I am choosing this Parish in a special way and I want to guide it." She emphasized this once again when she said," I am choosing this Parish in a special way, which is dearer to me than others, where I joyfully went when the Almighty sent me."(25th March 1985). Our Lady gave a reason too for her choice saying: "Convert, you in the Parish, this is my second wish. In that way, all those who come here will convert."(8th March 1984)." I am asking you, especially the members of this Parish, to live my messages"(16th August 1984). First of all the parishioners and the pilgrims should become witnesses of her apparitions, and her messages, so that we can then unite with her and the visionaries in the realization of her plan for conversion of the world and reconciliation with God.

Our Lady well knows the weaknesses and the nature of the parishioners and pilgrims with whom she wishes to collaborate in the salvation of the world. She is aware of the need for supernatural strength. That's why she leads them to the fount of that strength. This primarily is prayer. She ardently and continuously exhorts us to pray. Of all prayer, she especially stresses the Holy Mass, (7th March 1985, 16th May 1985) and recommends continuous devotion to the Blessed Sacrament (15th March 1984). She also encourages devotion to the Holy Spirit (2nd June 1984; 9th June 1984; 11th April 1985; 23rd May 1988, etc.) and the reading of Sacred Scripture (8th Sept. 1984; 14th Feb. 1985).

With these special messages to the Parish and it's pilgrims, Our Lady wishes that the first messages, which in the beginning were intended for the whole world, are deepened, made more acceptable and understandable to others.

From the 25th of January 1987 Our Lady began to give the message on the 25th of every month instead of every Thursday, through the visionary Marija Pavlović. This still continues today.

Weekly and Monthly Messages
March 1st 1984 to November 25th 2014

March 1, 1984

"Dear children! I have chosen this parish in a special way and I wish to lead it. I am guarding it in love and I want everyone to be mine. Thank you for having responded tonight. I wish you always to be with me and my Son in ever greater numbers. I shall speak a message to you every Thursday."

March 8, 1984

"Thank you for having responded to my call! Dear children, you in the parish, be converted. This is my other wish. That way all those who shall come here shall be able to convert."

March 15, 1984

"Tonight also, dear children, I am grateful to you in a special way for being here. Unceasingly adore the Most Blessed Sacrament of the Altar. I am always present when the faithful are adoring. Special graces are then being received."

March 22, 1984

"Dear children! In a special way this evening I am calling you during Lent to honor the wounds of my Son, which He received from the sins of this parish. Unite yourselves with my prayers for the parish so that His sufferings may be bearable. Thank you for having responded to my call. Try to come in ever greater numbers."

March 29, 1984

"Dear children! In a special way this evening I am calling you to perseverance in trials. Consider how the Almighty is still suffering today on account of your sins. So when sufferings come, offer them up as a sacrifice to God. Thank you for having responded to my call."

April 5, 1984

"Dear children! This evening I pray you especially to venerate the Heart of my Son, Jesus. Make reparation for the wound inflicted on the Heart of my Son. That Heart is offended by all kinds of sins. Thank you for coming this evening."

April 12, 1984

"Dear children! Today I beseech you to stop slandering and to pray for the unity of the parish, because I and my Son have a special plan for this parish. Thank you for having responded to my call."

April 19, 1984 (Holy Thursday)

"Dear children! Sympathise with me! Pray, pray, pray!"

April 26, 1984

No message.

April 30, 1984 (Monday)

Marija asked Our Lady, "Dear Madonna, why didn't you give me a message for the parish on Thursday?" Our Lady replied, "I do not wish to force anyone to do that which he/she neither feels nor desires, even though I had special messages for the parish by which I wanted to awaken the faith of every believer. But only a really small number has accepted my Thursday messages. In the beginning there were quite a few. But its become a routine affair for them. And now recently some are asking for the message out of curiosity, and not out of faith and devotion to my Son and me."

May 10, 1984

Many of the faithful felt shaken by the last message of Our Lady. Some had the feeling that Our Lady would not give any more messages to the parish, but this evening she said, "I am speaking to you and I wish to speak further. You just listen to my instructions!"

May 17, 1984

"Dear children! Today I am very happy because there are many who want to consecrate themselves to me. Thank you. You have not made a mistake. My Son, Jesus Christ, wishes to bestow on you special graces through me. My Son is happy because of your dedication. Thank you for having responded to my call."

May 24, 1984

"Dear children! I have told you already that I have chosen you in a special way, just the way you are. I, the Mother, love you all. And in any moment that is difficult for you, do not be afraid! Because I love you even then when you are far from me and my Son. Please, do not let my heart weep with tears of blood because of the souls who are lost in sin. Therefore, dear children, pray, pray, pray! Thank you for having responded to my call."

May 31, 1984 (Ascension Thursday)

There were many people present from abroad. Our Lady did not give a message for the parish. She told Marija that she would give a message on Saturday to be announced at the Sunday parish Mass.

June 2, 1984 (Saturday)

"Dear children! Tonight I wish to tell you during the days of this novena to pray for the outpouring of the Holy Spirit on your families and on your parish. Pray, and you shall not regret it. God will give you gifts by which you will glorify Him till the end of your life on this earth. Thank you for having responded to my call."

June 9, 1984 (Saturday)

"Dear children! Tomorrow night pray for the Spirit of Truth! Especially, you from the parish. Because you need the Spirit of Truth to be able to convey the messages just the way they are, neither adding anything to them, nor taking anything whatsoever away from them, but just the way I said them. Pray for the Holy Spirit to inspire you with the spirit of prayer, so you will pray more. I, your Mother, tell you that you are praying little. Thank you for having responded to my call."

June 14, 1984

No message.

June 21, 1984

"Pray, pray, pray! Thank you for having responded to my call."

June 28, 1984

No message was given by Our Lady

July 12, 1984

"Dear children! These days Satan wants to frustrate my plans. Pray that his plan not be realised. I will pray my Son Jesus to give you the grace to experience the victory of Jesus in the temptations of Satan. Thank you for having responded to my call."

July 19, 1984

"Dear children! These days you have been experiencing how Satan is working. I am always with you, and don't you be afraid of temptations because God is always watching over us. Also I have given myself to you and I sympathise with you even in the smallest temptation. Thank you for having responded to my call."

July 26, 1984

"Dear children! Today also I wish to call you to persistent prayer and penance. Especially, let the young people of this parish be more active in their prayers. Thank you for having responded to my call."

August 2, 1984

"Dear children! Today I am joyful and I thank you for your prayers. Pray still more these days for the conversion of sinners. Thank you for having responded to my call."

August 9, 1984

No message was given by Our Lady

August 11, 1984 (Saturday)

"Dear children! Pray, because Satan wishes to complicate my plans still further. Pray with the heart and surrender yourselves to Jesus in prayer."

August 14, 1984 (Tuesday)

This apparition was unexpected. Ivan was praying at home. After that he started to get ready to go to Church for the evening services. By surprise Our Lady appeared to him and told him to relate to the people. "I would like the people to pray along with me these days. And to pray as much as possible! And to fast strictly on Wednesdays and Fridays, and every day to pray at least one Rosary: the joyful, sorrowful and glorious mysteries." Our Lady asked that we accept this message with a firm will. She especially requested this of the parishioners and the faithful of the surrounding places.

August 16, 1984

"Dear children! I beseech you, especially those from this parish, to live my messages and convey them to others, to whomever you meet. Thank you for having responded to my call."

August 23, 1984

"Dear children! Pray, pray!" Marija said that She also invited the people, and especially the young people, to keep order during the Mass.

August 30, 1984

"Dear children! The cross was also in God's plan when you built it. These days, especially, go on the mountain and pray before the cross. I need your prayers. Thank you for having responded to my call."

September 6, 1984

"Dear children! Without prayer there is no peace. Therefore I say to you, dear children, pray at the foot of the cross for peace. Thank you for having responded to my call."

September 13, 1984

"Dear children! I still need your prayers. You wonder why all these prayers? Look around you, dear children, and you will see how greatly sin has dominated the world. Pray, therefore, that Jesus conquers. Thank you for having responded to my call."

September 20, 1984

"Dear children! Today I call on you to begin fasting with the heart. There are many people who are fasting, but only because everyone else is fasting. It has become a custom which no one wants to stop. I ask the parish to fast out of gratitude because God has allowed me to stay this long in this parish. Dear children, fast and pray with the heart. Thank you for having responded to my call."

September 27, 1984

"Dear children! You have helped me along by your prayers to realise my plans. Keep on praying that my plans are completed. I request the families of the parish to pray the family rosary. Thank you for having responded to my call."

October 4, 1984

"Dear children! Today I want to tell you that again and again you make me happy by your prayer, but there are enough of those in this very parish who do not pray and my heart is saddened. Therefore pray that I can bring all your sacrifices and prayers to the Lord. Thank you for having responded to my call."

October 8, 1984 (Monday)

(Jakov was sick and received this message at home.) "Dear children, Let all the prayers you say in your homes in the evening be for the conversion of sinners because the world is in great sin. Every evening pray the rosary."

October 11, 1984

"Dear children! Thank you for dedicating all your hard work to God even now when He is testing you through the grapes you are picking. Be assured, dear children, that He loves you and, therefore, He tests you. You just always offer up all your burdens to God and do not be anxious. Thank you for having responded to my call."

October 18, 1984

"Dear children! Today I call on you to read the Bible every day in your homes and let it be in a visible place so as always to encourage you to read it and to pray. Thank you for having responded to my call."

October 25, 1984

"Dear children! Pray during this month. God allows me every day to help you with graces to defend yourselves against evil. This is my month. I want to give it to you. You just pray and God will give you the graces you are seeking. I will help along with it. Thank you for having responded to my call."

November 1, 1984

"Dear children! Today I call you to the renewal of prayer in your homes. The work in the fields is over. Now devote yourselves to prayer. Let prayer take the first place in your families. Thank you for having responded to my call."

November 8, 1984

"Dear children! You are not conscious of the messages which God is sending you through me. He is giving you great graces and you do not comprehend them. Pray to the Holy Spirit for enlightenment. If you only knew how great are the graces God is granting you, you would be praying without ceasing. Thank you for having responded to my call."

November 15, 1984

"Dear children! You are a chosen people and God has given you great graces. You are not conscious of every message which I am giving you. Now I just want to say - pray, pray, pray! I don't know what else to tell you because I love you and I want you to comprehend my love and God's love through prayer. Thank you for having responded to my call."

November 22, 1984

"Dear children! These days live all the main messages and keep rooting them in your hearts till Thursday. Thank you for having responded to my call."

November 29, 1984

"Dear children! No, you don't know how to love and you don't know how to listen with love to the words I am saying to you. Be conscious, my beloved, that I am your Mother and I have come on earth to teach you to listen out of love, to pray out of love and not compelled by the fact that you are carrying a cross. By means of the cross God is glorified through every person. Thank you for having responded to my call."

December 6, 1984

"Dear children! These days I am calling you to family prayer. In God's Name many times I have been giving you messages, but you have not listened to me. This Christmas will be unforgettable for you only if you accept the messages which I am giving you. Dear children, don't allow that day of joy to become my most sorrowful day. Thank you for having responded to my call."

December 13, 1984

"Dear children! You know that the season of joy is getting closer, but without love you will achieve nothing. So first of all, begin to love your own family, everyone in the parish, and then you'll be able to love and accept all who are coming over here. Now let these seven days be a week when you need to learn to love. Thank you for having responded to my call."

December 20, 1984

"Dear children! Today I am inviting you to do something concrete for Jesus Christ. As a sign of dedication to Jesus I want each family of the parish to bring a single flower before that happy day. I want every member of the family to have a single flower by the crib so Jesus can come and see your dedication to Him! Thank you for having responded to my call."

December 21, 1984 (Friday)

"I want you to be a flower which will blossom for Jesus on Christmas. And a flower that will not stop blooming when Christmas is over. I want your hearts to be shepherds to Jesus."

(Message given through Jelena Vasilj.) [Dec. 21]

December 27, 1984

"Dear children! This Christmas Satan wanted in a special way to spoil God's plans. You, dear children, have discerned Satan even on Christmas day itself. But God is winning in all your hearts. So let your hearts keep on being happy. Thank you for having responded to my call."

1985

January 3, 1985

"Dear children! These days the Lord has bestowed upon you great graces. Let this week be one of thanksgiving for all the graces which God has granted you. Thank you for having responded to my call."

January 10, 1985

"Dear children! Today I want to thank you for all your sacrifices, but special thanks to those who have become dear to my heart and come here gladly[.] [There] are enough parishioners who are not listening to the messages, but because of those who are in a special way close to my heart, because of them I am giving messages for the parish. And I will go on giving them because I love you and I want you to spread my messages with your heart. Thank you for having responded to my call."

January 14, 1985 (Monday)

"My dear children! Satan is so strong and with all his might wants to disturb my plans which I have begun with you. You pray, just pray and don't stop for a minute! I will pray to my Son for the realisation of all the plans I have begun. Be patient and constant in your prayers. And don't let Satan discourage you. He is working hard in the world. Be on your guard!"

(Message conveyed by Vicka from Our Lady.)

January 17, 1985

"Dear children! These days Satan is working underhandedly against this parish, and you, dear children, have fallen asleep in prayer, and only some are going to Mass. Withstand the days of temptation! Thank you for having responded to my call."

January 24, 1985

"Dear children! These days you have experienced God's sweetness through the renewals which have been in this parish. Satan wants to work still more fiercely to take away your joy from each one of you. By prayer you can completely disarm him and ensure your happiness. Thank you for having responded to my call."

January 31, 1985

"Dear children! Today I wish to tell you to open your hearts to God like the spring flowers which crave for the sun. I am your Mother and I always want you to be closer to the Father and that He will always give abundant gifts to your hearts. Thank you for having responded to my call."

February 7, 1985

"Dear children! These days Satan is manifesting himself in a special way in this parish. Pray, dear children, that God's plan is brought into effect and that every work of Satan ends up for the glory of God. I have stayed with you this long so I might help you along in your trials. Thank you for having responded to my call."

February 14, 1985

"Dear children! Today is the day when I give you a message for the parish, but the whole parish is not accepting the messages and is not living them. I am saddened and I want you, dear children, to listen to me and to live my messages. Every family must pray family prayer and read the Bible! Thank you for having responded to my call."

February 21, 1985

"Dear children! From day to day I have been inviting you to renewal and prayer in the parish, but you are not accepting it. Today I am calling you for the last time! Now it's Lent and you as a parish can turn to my messages during Lent out of love. If you do not do that, I do not wish to keep on giving messages. God is permitting me that. Thank you for having responded to my call."

February 28, 1985

"Dear children! Today I call you to live the word this week: "I love God!" Dear children through love you will achieve everything and even what you think is impossible. God wants this parish to belong completely to Him. And that's what I want too. Thank you for having responded to my call."

March 7, 1985

"Dear children! Today I call you to renew prayer in your families. Dear children, encourage the very young to prayer and the children to go to Holy Mass. Thank you for having responded to my call."

March 14, 1985

"Dear children! In your life you have all experienced light and darkness. God grants to every person to recognize good and evil. I am calling you to the light which you should carry to all the people who are in darkness. People who are in darkness daily come into your homes. Dear children, give them the light! Thank you for having responded to my call."

March 21, 1985

"Dear children! I wish to keep on giving messages and therefore today I call you to live and accept my messages! Dear children, I love you and in a special way I have chosen this parish, one more dear to me than the others, in which I have gladly remained when the Almighty sent me. Therefore I call on you - accept me, dear children, that it might go well with you. Listen to my messages! Thank you for having responded to my call."

March 24, 1985 (Sunday)

"Today I wish to call you all to confession, even if you have confessed a few days ago. I wish that you all experience my feast day within yourselves. But you cannot experience it unless you abandon yourselves completely to God. Therefore, I am inviting you all to reconciliation with God!"

March 28, 1985

"Dear children! Today I wish to call you to pray, pray, pray! In prayer you shall perceive the greatest joy and the way out of every situation that has no exit. Thank you for starting up prayer. Each individual is dear to my heart. And I thank all who have urged prayer in their families. Thank you for having responded to my call."

April 4, 1985 (Holy Thursday)

"Dear children! I thank you for having started to think more about God's glory in your hearts.

Today is the day when I wished to stop giving the messages because some individuals did not accept me. The parish has been moved and I wish to keep on giving you messages as it has never been in history from the beginning of the world. Thank you for having responded to my call."

April 5, 1985 (Good Friday)

"You parishioners have a great and heavy cross, but don't be afraid to carry it. My Son is here who will help you."

(Message given through Ivanka)

April 11, 1985

"Dear children! Today I wish to say to everyone in the parish to pray in a special way to the Holy Spirit for enlightenment. From today God wishes to test the parish in a special way in order that He might strengthen it in faith. Thank you for having responded to my call."

April 18, 1985

"Dear children! Today I thank you for every opening of your hearts. Joy overtakes me for every heart that is opened to God especially from the parish. Rejoice with me! Pray all the prayers for the opening of sinful hearts. I desire that. God desires that through me. Thank you for having responded to my call."

April 25, 1985

"Dear children! Today I wish to tell you to begin to work in your hearts as you are working in the fields. Work and change your hearts so that a new spirit from God can take its place in your hearts. Thank you for having responded to my call."

May 2, 1985

"Dear children! Today I call you to prayer with the heart, and not just from habit. Some are coming but do not wish to move ahead in prayer. Therefore, I wish to warn you like a Mother: pray that prayer prevails in your hearts in every moment. Thank you for having responded to my call."

May 9, 1985

"Dear children! No, you do not know how many graces God is giving you. You do not want to move ahead during these days when the Holy Spirit is working in a special way. Your hearts are turned toward the things of earth and they preoccupy you. Turn your hearts toward prayer and seek the Holy Spirit to be poured out on you. Thank you for having responded to my call."

May 16, 1985

"Dear children! I am calling you to a more active prayer and attendance at Holy Mass. I wish your Mass to be an experience of God. I wish especially to say to the young people: be open to the Holy Spirit because God wishes to draw you to Himself in these days when Satan is at work. Thank you for having responded to my call."

May 23, 1985

"Dear children! These days I call you especially to open your hearts to the Holy Spirit. Especially during these days the Holy Spirit is working through you. Open your hearts and surrender your life to Jesus so that He works through your hearts and strengthens you in faith. Thank you for having responded to my call."

May 30, 1985

"Dear children! I call you again to prayer with the heart. Let prayer, dear children, be your every day food in a special way when your work in the fields is so wearing you out that you cannot pray with the heart. Pray, and then you shall overcome even every weariness. Prayer will be your joy and your rest. Thank you for having responded to my call."

June 6, 1985

"Dear children! During these days people from all nations will be coming into the parish. And now I am calling you to love: love first of all your own household members, and then you will be able to accept and love all who are coming. Thank you for having responded to my call."

June 13, 1985

"Dear children! Until the anniversary day I am calling you, the parish, to pray more and to let your prayer be a sign of surrender to God. Dear children, I know that you are all tired, but you don't know how to surrender yourselves to me. During these days surrender yourselves completely to me! Thank your for having responded to my call."

June 20, 1985

Dear children! For this Feast Day I wish to tell you to open your hearts to the Master of all hearts.

Give me all your feelings and all your problems! I wish to comfort you in all your trials. I wish to fill you with peace, joy and love of God. Thank you for having responded to my call."

June 25, 1985 (Tuesday)

"I invite you to call on everyone to pray the Rosary. With the Rosary you shall overcome all the adversities which Satan is trying to inflict on the Catholic Church. All you priests, pray the Rosary! Dedicate your time to the Rosary!" (This message Our Lady gave in response to the question of Marija Pavlović: "Our Lady, what do you wish to recommend to priests?")

June 28, 1985 (Friday)

"Dear children! Today I am giving you a message through which I desire to call you to humility. These days you have felt great joy because of all the people who have come and to whom you could tell your experiences with love. Now I invite you to continue in humility and with an open heart speak to all who are coming. Thank you for having responded to my message."

July 4, 1985

"Dear children! I thank you for every sacrifice you have offered. And now I urge you to offer every sacrifice with love. I wish you, the helpless ones, to begin helping with confidence and the Lord will keep on giving to you in confidence. Thank you for having responded to my call."

July 11, 1985

"Dear children! I love the parish and with my mantle I protect it from every work of Satan. Pray that Satan retreats from the parish and from every individual who comes into the parish. In that way you shall be able to hear every call of God and answer it with your life. Thank you for having responded to my call."

July 18, 1985

"Dear children! Today I call you to place more blessed objects in your homes and that everyone put some blessed objects on their person. Bless all the objects and thus Satan will attack you less because you will have armour against him. Thank you for having responded to my call."

July 25, 1985

"Dear children! I desire to lead you, but you do not wish to listen to my messages. Today I am calling you to listen to the messages and then you will be able to live everything which God tells me to convey to you. Open yourselves to God and God will work through you and keep on giving you everything you need. Thank you for having responded to my call."

August 1, 1985

"Dear children! I wish to tell you that I have chosen this parish and that I am guarding it in my hands like a little flower that does not want to die. I call you to surrender to me so that I can keep on presenting you to God, fresh and without sin. Satan has taken part of the plan and wants to possess it. Pray that he does not succeed in that, because I wish you for myself so I can keep on giving you to God. Thank you for having responded to my call."

August 8, 1985

"Dear children! Today I call you especially now to advance against Satan by means of prayer. Satan wants to work still more now that you know he is at work. Dear children, put on the armour for battle and with the Rosary in your hand defeat him! Thank you for having responded to my call."

August 15, 1985

"Dear children! Today I am blessing you and I wish to tell you that I love you and that I urge you to live my messages. Today I am blessing you with the solemn blessing that the Almighty grants me. Thank you for having responded to my call."

August 22, 1985

"Dear children! Today I wish to tell you that God wants to send you trials which you can overcome by prayer. God is testing you through daily chores. Now pray to peacefully withstand every trial. From everything through which God tests you come out more open to God and approach Him with love. Thank you for having responded to my call."

August 29, 1985

"Dear children! I am calling you to prayer! Especially since Satan wishes to take advantage of the yield of your vineyards. Pray that Satan does not succeed in his plan. Thank you for having responded to my call."

September 5, 1985

"Dear children! Today I thank you for all the prayers. Keep on praying all the more so that Satan will be far away from this place. Dear children,

Satan's plan has failed. Pray for fulfillment of what God plans in this parish. I especially thank the young people for the sacrifices they have offered up. Thank you for having responded to my call."

September 12, 1985

"Dear children! I wish to tell you that the cross should be central these days. Pray especially before the cross from which great graces are coming. Now in your homes make a special consecration to the cross. Promise that you will neither offend Jesus nor abuse the cross. Thank you for having responded to my call."

September 19, 1985

No message.

September 20, 1985 (Friday)

"Dear children! Today I invite you to live in humility all the messages which I am giving you. Do not become arrogant living the messages and saying 'I am living the messages'. If you shall bear and live the messages in your heart, everyone will feel it so that words, which serve those who do not obey, will not be necessary. For you, dear children, it is necessary to live and witness by your lives. Thank you for having responded to my call."

September 26, 1985

"Dear children! I thank you for all the prayers. Thank you for all the sacrifices. I wish to tell you, dear children, to renew the messages which I am giving you. Especially live the fasting, because by fasting you will give me the joy of seeing fulfilled all the plans which God has here in Medjugorje. Thank you for having responded to my call."

October 3, 1985

"Dear children! I wish to tell you to thank God for all the graces which God has given you. For all the fruits thank the Lord and glorify him! Dear children, learn to give thanks in little things and then you will be able to give thanks also for the big things. Thank you for having responded to my call."

October 10, 1985

"Dear children! I wish also today to call you to live the messages in the parish. Especially I wish to call the youth of the parish, who are dear to me. Dear children, if you live the messages, you are living the seed of holiness. I, as the Mother, wish to call you all to holiness so that you can bestow it on others. You are a mirror to others! Thank you for having responded to my call."

October 17, 1985

"Dear children! Everything has its own time. Today I call you to start working on your own hearts. Now that all the work in the field is over, you are finding time for cleaning even the most neglected areas, but you leave your heart aside. Work more and clean with love every part of your heart. Thank you for having responded to my call."

October 24, 1985

"Dear children! From day to day I wish to clothe you in holiness, goodness, obedience and God's love, so that from day to day you become more beautiful and more prepared for your Master. Dear children, listen to and live my messages. I wish to guide you. Thank you for having responded to my call."

October 31, 1985

"Dear children! Today I wish to call you to work in the Church. I love all the same and I desire from each one to work as much as is possible. I know, dear children, that you can, but you do not wish to because you feel small and humble in these things. You need to be courageous and with little flowers do your share for the church and for Jesus so that everyone can be satisfied. Thank you for having responded to my call."

November 7, 1985

"Dear children! I am calling you to the love of neighbour and love toward the one from whom evil comes to you. In that way with love you will be able to discern the intentions of hearts. Pray and love, dear children! By love you are able to do even that which you think is impossible. Thank you for having responded to my call."

November 14, 1985

"Dear children! I, your Mother, love you and wish to urge you to prayer. I am tireless, dear children, and I am calling you even then, when you are far away from my heart. I am a Mother, and even though I feel pain for each one who goes astray, I forgive easily and am happy for every child who returns to me. Thank you for having responded to my call."

November 21, 1985

"Dear children! I want to tell you that this season is especially for you from the parish. When it is summer, you saw that you have a lot of work. Now you don't have work in the fields, work on your own self personally! Come to Mass because this is the season given to you. Dear children, there are enough of those who come regularly despite bad weather because they love me and wish to show their love in a special way. What I want from you is to show me your love by coming to Mass, and the Lord will reward you abundantly. Thank you for having responded to my call."

November 28, 1985

"Dear children! I want to thank everyone for all you have done for me, especially the youth. I beseech you, dear children, come to prayer with awareness. In prayer you shall come to know the greatness of God. Thank you for having responded to my call."

December 5, 1985

"Dear children! I am calling you to prepare yourselves for Christmas by means of penance, prayer and works of charity. Dear children, do not look towards material things, because then you will not be able to experience Christmas. Thank you for having responded to my call."

December 12, 1985

"Dear children! For Christmas my invitation is that together we glorify Jesus. I present Him to you in a special way on that day and my invitation to you is that on that day we glorify Jesus and His Nativity. Dear children, on that day pray still more and think more about Jesus. Thank you for having responded to my call."

December 19, 1985

"Dear children! Today I wish to call you to love of neighbour. The more you will to love your neighbour, the more you shall experience Jesus especially on Christmas Day. God will bestow great gifts on you if you surrender yourselves to Him. I wish in a special way on Christmas Day to give mothers my own special motherly blessing, and Jesus will bless the rest with His own blessing. Thank you for having responded to my call."

December 26, 1985

"Dear children! I wish to thank all who have listened to my messages and who on Christmas Day have lived what I said. Undefiled by sin from now on, I wish to lead you further in love. Abandon your hearts to me! Thank you for having responded to my call!"

1986

January 2, 1986

"Dear children! I call you to decide completely for God. I beseech you, dear children, to surrender yourselves completely and you shall be able to live everything I am telling you. It shall not be difficult for you to surrender yourselves completely to God. Thank you for having responded to my call."

January 9, 1986

"Dear children! I call you by your prayers to help Jesus along in the fulfillment of all the plans which He is forming here. And offer your sacrifices to Jesus in order that everything is fulfilled the way He has planned it and that Satan can accomplish nothing. Thank you for having responded to my call."

January 16, 1986

"Dear children! Today also I am calling you to prayer. Your prayers are necessary to me so that God may be glorified through all of you. Dear children, I pray you, obey and live the Mother's invitation, because only out of love am I calling you in order that I might help you. Thank you for having responded to my call."

January 23, 1986

"Dear children! Again I call you to prayer with the heart. If you pray with the heart, dear children, the ice of your brothers will melt and every barrier shall disappear. Conversion will be easy for all who desire to accept it. That is the gift which by prayer you must obtain for your neighbour. Thank you for having responded to my call."

January 30, 1986

"Dear children! Today I call you all to pray that God's plans for us may be realised and also everything that God desires through you! Help others to be converted, especially those who are coming to Medjugorje. Dear children, do not allow Satan to get control of your hearts, so you would be an image of Satan and not of me. I call you to pray for how you might be witnesses of my presence. Without you, God cannot bring to reality that which He desires. God has given a free will to everyone, and it's in your control. Thank you for having responded to my call."

February 6, 1986

"Dear children! This parish, which I have chosen, is special and different from others. And I am giving great graces to all who pray with the heart. Dear children, I am giving the messages first of all to the residents of the parish, and then to all the others. First of all you must accept the messages, and then the others. You shall be answerable to me and my Son, Jesus. Thank you for having responded to my call."

February 13, 1986

"Dear children! This Lent is a special incentive for you to change. Start from this moment. Turn off the television and renounce various things that are of no value. Dear children, I am calling you individually to conversion. This season is for you. Thank you for having responded to my call."

February 20, 1986

"Dear children! The second message of these Lenten days is that you renew prayer before the cross. Dear children, I am giving you special graces and Jesus is giving you special gifts from the cross. Take them and live! Reflect on Jesus' Passion and in your life be united with Jesus! Thank you for having responded to my call."

February 27, 1986

"Dear children! In humility live the messages which I am giving you. Thank you for having responded to my call."

March 6, 1986

"Dear children! Today I call you to open yourselves more to God, so that He can work through you. The more you open yourselves, the more you receive the fruits. I wish to call you again to prayer. Thank you for having responded to my call."

March 13, 1986

"Dear children! Today I call you to live Lent by means of your little sacrifices. Thank you for every sacrifice you have brought me. Dear children, live that way continuously, and with your love help me to present the sacrifice. God will reward you for that. Thank you for having responded to my call."

March 20, 1986

"Dear children! Today I call you to approach prayer actively. You wish to live everything I am telling you, but you are not succeeding because you are not praying. Dear children, I beseech you to open yourselves and begin to pray. Prayer will be your joy. If you make a start, it won't be boring to you because you will be praying out of joy. Thank you for having responded to my call."

March 27, 1986

"Dear children! I wish to thank you for all the sacrifices and I invite you to the greatest sacrifice, the sacrifice of love. Without love, you are not able to accept either me or my Son. Without love, you cannot give an account of your experiences to others. Therefore, dear children, I call you to begin to live love within yourselves. Thank you for having responded to my call."

April 3, 1986

"Dear children! I wish to call you to a living of the Holy Mass. There are many of you who have sensed the beauty of the Holy Mass, but there are also those who come unwillingly. I have chosen you, dear children, but Jesus gives you His graces in the Mass. Therefore, consciously live the Holy Mass and let your coming to it be a joyful one. Come to it with love and make the Mass your own. Thank you for having responded to my call."

April 10, 1986

"Dear children! I desire to call you to grow in love. A flower is not able to grow normally without water. So also you, dear children, are not able to grow without God's blessing. From day to day you need to seek His blessing so you will grow normally and perform all your actions in union with God. Thank you for having responded to my call."

April 17, 1986

"Dear children! You are absorbed with material things, but in the material you lose everything that God wishes to give you. I call you, dear children, to pray for the gifts of the Holy Spirit which are necessary for you now in order to be able to give witness to my presence here and to all that I am giving you. Dear children, let go to me so I can lead you completely. Don't be absorbed with material things. Thank you for having responded to my call."

April 24, 1986

"Dear children! Today my invitation is that you pray. Dear children, you are forgetting that you are all important. The elderly are especially important in the family. Urge them to pray. Let all the young people be an example to others by their life and let them witness to Jesus. Dear children, I beseech you, begin to change through prayer and you will know what you need to do. Thank you for having responded to my call."

May 1, 1986

"Dear children! I beseech you to start changing your life in the family. Let the family be a harmonious flower that I wish to give to Jesus. Dear children, let every family be active in prayer for I wish that the fruits in the family be seen one day. Only that way shall I give you all, like petals, as a gift to Jesus in fulfillment of God's plans. Thank you for having responded to my call."

May 8, 1986

"Dear children! You are the ones responsible for the messages. The source of grace is here, but you, dear children, are the vessels which transport the gifts. Therefore, dear children, I am calling you to do your job with responsibility. Each one shall be responsible according to his own ability. Dear children, I am calling you to give the gifts to others with love, and not to keep them for yourselves. Thank you for having responded to my call."

May 15, 1986

"Dear children! Today I call you to give me your heart so I can change it to be like mine. You are wondering, dear children, why you cannot respond to that which I am seeking from you. You are not able to because you have not given me your heart so I can change it. You are talking but you are not doing. I call on you to do everything that I am telling you. That way I will be with you. Thank you for having responded to my call."

May 22, 1986

"Dear children! Today I wish to give you my own love. You do not know, dear children, how great my love is, and you do not know how to accept it. In various ways I wish to show it to you, but you, dear children, do not recognize it. You do not understand my words with your heart and neither are you able to comprehend my love. Dear children, accept me in your life and so you will be able to accept all I am saying to you and to which I am calling you. Thank you for having responded to my call."

May 29, 1986

"Dear children! Today my call to you is that in your life you live love towards God and neighbour. Without love, dear children, you can do nothing. Therefore, dear children, I am calling you to live in mutual love. Only in that way will you be able to love and accept both me and all those around you who are coming into your parish. Everyone will sense my love through you. Therefore, I beseech you, dear children, to start loving from today with an ardent love, the love with which I love you. Thank you for having responded to my call."

June 5, 1986

"Dear children! Today I am calling on you to decide whether or not you wish to live the messages which I am giving you. I wish you to be active in living and spreading the messages. Especially, dear children, I wish that you all be the reflection of Jesus, which will enlighten this unfaithful world walking in darkness. I wish all of you to be the light for everyone and that you give witness in the light. Dear children, you are not called to the darkness, but you are called to the light. Therefore, live the light with your own life. Thank you for having responded to my call."

June 12, 1986

"Dear children! Today I call you to begin to pray the Rosary with a living faith. That way I will be able to help you. You, dear children, wish to obtain graces, but you are not praying. I am not able to help you because you do not want to get started. Dear children, I am calling you to pray the Rosary and that your Rosary be an obligation which you shall fulfill with joy. That way you shall understand the reason I am with you this long. I desire to teach you to pray. Thank you for having responded to my call."

June 19, 1986

"Dear children! During these days my Lord is allowing me to be able to intercede more graces for you. Therefore, I wish to urge you once more to pray, dear children! Pray without ceasing! That way I will give you the joy which the Lord gives to me. With these graces, dear children, I want your sufferings to be a joy. I am your Mother and I desire to help you. Thank you for having responded to my call."

June 26, 1986

"Dear children! God is allowing me along with Himself to bring about this oasis of peace. I wish to call on you to protect it and that the oasis always be unspoiled. There are those who by their carelessness are destroying the peace and the prayer. I am inviting you to give witness and by your own life to help to preserve the peace. Thank you for having responded to my call."

July 3, 1986

"Dear children! Today I am calling you all to prayer. Without prayer, dear children, you are not able to experience either God, or me or the graces which I am giving you. Therefore, my call to you is that the beginning and end of your day always be prayer. Dear children, I wish to lead you daily more and more in prayer, but you are not able to grow because you do not desire it. My call, dear children, is that for you prayer be in the first place. Thank you for having responded to my call."

July 10, 1986

"Dear children! Today I am calling you to holiness. Without holiness you cannot live. Therefore, with love overcome every sin and with love overcome all the difficulties which are coming to you. Dear children, I beseech you to live love within yourselves. Thank you for having responded to my call."

July 17, 1986

"Dear children! Today I am calling you to reflect upon why I am with you this long. I am the Mediatrix between you and God. Therefore, dear children, I desire to call you to live always out of love all that which God desires of you. For that reason, dear children, in your own humility live all the messages which I am giving you. Thank you for having responded to my call."

July 24, 1986

"Dear children! I rejoice because of all of you who are on the way of holiness and I beseech you, by your own testimony help those who do not know how to live in holiness. Therefore, dear children, let your family be a place where holiness is birthed. Help everyone to live in holiness, but especially your own family. Thank you for having responded to my call."

July 31, 1986

"Dear children! Hatred gives birth to dissensions and does not regard anyone or anything. I call you always to bring harmony and peace. Especially, dear children, in the place where you live, act with love. Let your only instrument always be love. By love turn everything into good which Satan desires to destroy and possess. Only that way shall you be completely mine and I shall be able to help you. Thank you for having responded to my call."

August 7, 1986

"Dear children! You know that I promised you an oasis of peace, but you don't know that beside an oasis stands the desert, where Satan is lurking and wanting to tempt each one of you. Dear children, only by prayer are you able to overcome every influence of Satan in your place. I am with you, but I cannot take away your freedom. Thank you for having responded to my call."

August 14, 1986

"Dear children! My call to you is that your prayer be the joy of an encounter with the Lord. I am not able to guide you as long as you yourselves do not experience joy in prayer. From day to day I desire to lead you more and more in prayer, but I do not wish to force you. Thank you for having responded to my call."

August 21, 1986

"Dear children! I thank you for the love which you are showing me. You know, dear children, that I love you immeasurably and daily I pray the Lord to help you to understand the love which I am showing you. Therefore, you, dear children, pray, pray, pray!"

August 28, 1986

"Dear children! My call is that in everything you would be an image for others, especially in prayer and witnessing. Dear children, without you I am not able to help the world. I desire that you cooperate with me in everything, even in the smallest things. Therefore, dear children, help me by letting your prayer be from the heart and all of you surrendering completely to me. That way I shall be able to teach and lead you on this way which I have begun with you. Thank you for having responded to my call."

September 4, 1986

"Dear children! Today again I am calling you to prayer and fasting. You know, dear children, that with your help I am able to accomplish everything and force Satan not to be seducing to evil and to remove himself from this place. Dear children, Satan is lurking for each individual. Especially in everyday affairs he wants to spread confusion among each one of you. Therefore, dear children, my call to you is that your day would be only prayer and complete surrender to God. Thank you for having responded to my call."

September 11, 1986

"Dear children! For these days while you are joyfully celebrating the cross, I desire that your cross also would be a joy for you. Especially, dear children, pray that you may be able to accept sickness and suffering with love the way Jesus accepted them. Only that way shall I be able with joy to give out to you the graces and healings which Jesus is permitting me. Thank you for having responded to my call."

September 18, 1986

"Dear children! Today again I thank you for all that you have accomplished for me in these days. Especially, dear children, I thank you in the Name of Jesus for the sacrifices which you offered in this past week. Dear children, you are forgetting that I desire sacrifices from you so I can help you and drive Satan away from you. Therefore, I am calling you again to offer sacrifices with a special reverence toward God. Thank you for having responded to my call."

September 25, 1986

"Dear children! By your own peace I am calling you to help others to see and begin to seek peace. You, dear children, are at peace and not able to comprehend lack of peace. Therefore, I am calling you, so that by your prayer and your life you help to destroy everything that is evil in people and uncover the deception that Satan makes use of. You pray that the truth prevails in all hearts. Thank you for having responded to my call."

October 2, 1986

"Dear children! Today again I am calling you to pray. You, dear children, are not able to understand how great the value of prayer is as long as you yourselves do not say: 'now is the time for prayer, now nothing else is important to me, now not one person is important to me but God.' Dear children, consecrate yourselves to prayer with a special love so that God will be able to render graces back to you. Thank you for having responded to my call."

October 9, 1986

"Dear children! You know that I desire to lead you on the way of holiness, but I do not want to compel you to be saints by force. I desire that each of you by your own little self-denials help yourself and me so I can lead you from day to day closer to holiness. Therefore, dear children, I do not desire to force you to observe the messages. But rather this long time that I am with you is a sign that I love you immeasurably and what I desire of each individual is to become holy. Thank you for having responded to my call."

October 16, 1986

"Dear children! Today again I want to show you how much I love you, but I am sorry that I am not able to help each one to understand my love. Therefore, dear children, I am calling you to prayer and complete surrender to God, because Satan wants to sift you through everyday affairs and in your life he wants to snatch the first place. Therefore, dear children, pray without ceasing! Thank you for having responded to my call."

October 23, 1986

"Dear children! Today again I am calling you to pray. Especially, dear children, do I call you to pray for peace. Without your prayers, dear children, I cannot help you to fulfill the message which the Lord has given me to give to you.

Therefore, dear children, pray, so that in prayer you realise what God is giving you. Thank you for having responded to my call."

October 30, 1986

"Dear children! Today again I desire to call you to take seriously and carry out the messages which I am giving you. Dear children, it is for your sake that I have stayed this long so I could help you to fulfill all the messages which I am giving you. Therefore, dear children, out of love for me carry out all the messages which I am giving you. Thank you for having responded to my call."

November 6, 1986

"Dear children! Today I wish to call you to pray daily for souls in purgatory. For every soul prayer and grace is necessary to reach God and the love of God. By doing this, dear children, you obtain new intercessors who will help you in life to realize that all the earthly things are not important for you, that only Heaven is that for which it is necessary to strive. Therefore, dear children, pray without ceasing that you may be able to help yourselves and the others to whom your prayers will bring joy. Thank you for having responded to my call."

November 13, 1986

"Dear children! Today again I am calling you to pray with your whole heart and day by day to change your life. Especially, dear children, I am calling that by your prayers and sacrifices you begin to live in holiness, because I desire that each one of you who has been to this fountain of grace will come to Paradise with the special gift which you shall give me, and that is holiness. Therefore, dear children, pray and daily change your life in order to become fully holy. I shall always be close to you. Thank you for having responded to my call."

November 20, 1986

"Dear children! Today also I am calling you to live and follow with a special love all the messages which I am giving you. Dear children, God does not want you lukewarm and undecided, but that you totally surrender to Him. You know that I love you and that out of love I long for you. Therefore, dear children, you also decide for love so that you will long for and daily experience God's love. Dear children, decide for love so that love prevails in all of you, but not human love, rather God's love. Thank you for having responded to my call."

November 27, 1986

"Dear children! Again today I call you to consecrate your life to me with love, so I am able to guide you with love. I love you, dear children, with a special love and I desire to bring you all to Heaven unto God. I want you to realise that this life lasts briefly compared to the one in Heaven. Therefore, dear children, decide again today for God. Only that way will I be able to show how much you are dear to me and how much I desire all to be saved and to be with me in Heaven. Thank you for having responded to my call."

December 4, 1986

"Dear children! Today I call you to prepare your hearts for these days when the Lord particularly desires to purify you from all the sins of your past. You, dear children, are not able by yourselves, therefore I am here to help you. You pray, dear children! Only that way shall you be able to recognize all the evil that is in you and surrender it to the Lord so the Lord may completely purify your hearts. Therefore, dear children, pray without ceasing and prepare your hearts in penance and fasting. Thank you for having responded to my call."

December 11, 1986

"Dear children! I am calling you to pray especially at this time in order to experience the joy of meeting with the new-born Jesus. Dear children, I desire that you experience these days just as I experience them. With joy I wish to guide you and show you the joy into which I desire to bring each one of you. Therefore, dear children, pray and surrender completely to me. Thank you for having responded to my call."

December 18, 1986

"Dear children! Once again I desire to call you to prayer. When you pray you are much more beautiful, like flowers, which after the snow, show all their beauty and all their colours become indescribable. So also you, dear children, after prayer show before God all so much more what is beautiful and are beloved by Him. Therefore, dear children, pray and open your inner self to

69

the Lord so that He makes of you a harmonious and beautiful flower for Paradise. Thank you for having responded to my call."

December 25, 1986 (Christmas Day)

"Dear children! Today also I give thanks to the Lord for all that He is doing for me, especially for this gift that I am able to be with you also today. Dear children, these are the days in which the Father grants special graces to all who open their hearts. I bless you and I desire that you too, dear children, become alive to the graces and place everything at God's disposal so that He may be glorified through you. My heart carefully follows your progress. Thank you for having responded to my call."

1987

January 1, 1987

"Dear children! Today I wish to call on all of you that in the New Year you live the messages which I am giving you. Dear children, you know that for your sake I have remained a long time so I might teach you how to make progress on the way of holiness. Therefore, dear children, pray without ceasing and live the messages which I am giving you for I am doing it with great love toward God and toward you. Thank you for having responded to my call."

January 8, 1987

"Dear children! I desire to thank you for every response to the messages. Especially, dear children, thank you for all the sacrifices and prayers which you have presented to me. Dear children, I desire to keep on giving you still further messages, only not every Thursday, dear children, but on each 25th in the month. The time has come when what my Lord desired has been fulfilled. Now I will give you less messages, but I am still with you. Therefore, dear children, I beseech you, listen to my messages and live them, so I can guide you. Dear children, thank you for having responded to my call."

MONTHLY MESSAGES

1987

January 25, 1987

"Dear children! Behold, also today I want to call you to start living a new life as of today. Dear children, I want you to comprehend that God has chosen each one of you, in order to use you in His great plan for the salvation of mankind. You are not able to comprehend how great your role is in God's design. Therefore, dear children, pray so that in prayer you may be able to comprehend what God's plan is in your regard. I am with you in order that you may be able to bring it about in all its fullness. Thank you for having responded to my call."

February 25, 1987

"Dear children! Today I want to wrap you all in my mantle and lead you all along the way of conversion. Dear children, I beseech you, surrender to the Lord your entire past, all the evil that has accumulated in your hearts. I want each one of you to be happy, but in sin nobody can be happy. Therefore, dear children, pray, and in prayer you shall realize a new way of joy. Joy will manifest in your hearts and thus you shall be joyful witnesses of that which I and My Son want from each one of you. I am blessing you. Thank you for having responded to my call."

March 25, 1987

"Dear children! Today I am grateful to you for your presence in this place, where I am giving you special graces. I call each one of you to begin to live as of today that life which God wishes of you and to begin to perform good works of love and mercy. I do not want you, dear children, to live the message and be committing sin which is displeasing to me. Therefore, dear children, I want each of you to live a new life without destroying all that God produces in you and is giving you. I give you my special blessing and I am remaining with you on your way of conversion. Thank you for having responded to my call."

April 25, 1987

"Dear children! Today also I am calling you to prayer. You know, dear children, that God grants special graces in prayer. Therefore, seek and pray in order that you may be able to comprehend all that I am giving here. I call you, dear children, to prayer with the heart. You know that without prayer you cannot comprehend all that God is planning through each one of you. Therefore, pray! I desire that through each one of you God's plan may be fulfilled, that all which God has planted in your heart may keep on growing. So pray that God's blessing may protect each one of you from all the evil that is threatening you. I bless you, dear children. Thank you for having responded to my call."

May 25, 1987

"Dear children! I am calling everyone of you to start living in God's love. Dear children, you are ready to commit sin, and to put yourselves in the hand of Satan without reflecting. I call on each one of you to consciously decide for God and against Satan. I am your Mother and, therefore, I want to lead you all to perfect holiness. I want each one of you to be happy here on earth and to be with me in Heaven. That is, dear children, the purpose of my coming here and it's my desire. Thank you for having responded to my call."

June 25, 1987

"Dear children! Today I thank you and I want to invite you all to God's peace. I want each one of you to experience in your heart that peace which God gives. I want to bless you all today. I am blessing you with God's blessing and I beseech you, dear children, to follow and to live my way. I love you, dear children, and so not even counting the number of times, I go on calling you and I thank you for all that you are doing for my intentions. I beg you, help me to present you to God and to save you. Thank you for having responded to my call."

July 25, 1987

"Dear children! I beseech you to take up the way of holiness beginning today. I love you and, therefore, I want you to be holy. I do not want Satan to block you on that way. Dear children, pray and accept all that God is offering you on a way which is bitter. But at the same time, God will reveal every sweetness to whomever begins to go on that way, and He will gladly answer every call of God. Do not attribute importance to petty things. Long for Heaven. Thank you for having responded to my call."

August 25, 1987

"Dear children! Today also I am calling you all in order that each one of you decides to live my messages. God has permitted me also in this year, which the Church has dedicated to me, to be able to speak to you and to be able to spur you on to holiness. Dear children, seek from God the graces which He is giving you through me. I am ready to intercede with God for all that you seek so that your holiness may be complete. Therefore, dear children, do not forget to seek, because God has permitted me to obtain graces for you. Thank you for having responded to my call."

September 25, 1987

"Dear children! Today also I want to call you all to prayer. Let prayer be your life. Dear children, dedicate your time only to Jesus and He will give you everything that you are seeking. He will reveal Himself to you in fullness. Dear children, Satan is strong and is waiting to test each one of you. Pray, and that way he will neither be able to injure you nor block you on the way of holiness. Dear children, through prayer grow all the more toward God from day to day. Thank you for having responded to my call."

October 25, 1987

"My dear children! Today I want to call all of you to decide for Paradise. The way is difficult for those who have not decided for God. Dear children, decide and believe that God is offering Himself to you in His fullness. You are invited and you need to answer the call of the Father, Who is calling you through me. Pray, because in prayer each one of you will be able to achieve complete love. I am blessing you and I desire to help you so that each one of you might be under my motherly mantle. Thank you for having responded to my call."

November 25, 1987

"Dear children! Today also I call each one of you to decide to surrender again everything completely to me. Only that way will I be able to present each of you to God. Dear children, you know that I love you immeasurably and that I desire each of you for myself, but God has given to all a freedom which I lovingly respect and humbly submit to. I desire, dear children, that you help so that everything God has planned in this parish shall be realised. If you do not pray, you shall not be able to recognize my love and the plans which God has for this parish and for each individual. Pray that Satan does not entice you with his pride and deceptive strength. I am with you and I want you to believe me, that I love you. Thank you for having responded to my call."

December 25, 1987

"Dear children! Rejoice with me! My heart is rejoicing because of Jesus and today I want to give Him to you. Dear children, I want each one of you to open your heart to Jesus and I will give Him to you with love. Dear children, I want Him to change you, to teach you and to protect you. Today I am praying in a special way for each one of you and I am presenting you to God so He will manifest Himself in you. I am calling you to sincere prayer with the heart so that every prayer of yours may be an encounter with God. In your work and in your everyday life, put God in the first place. I call you today with great seriousness to obey me and to do as I am calling you. Thank you for having responded to my call."

1988

January 25, 1988

"Dear children! Today again I am calling you to complete conversion, which is difficult for those who have not chosen God. God can give you everything that you seek from Him. But you seek God only when sicknesses, problems and difficulties come to you and you think that God is far from you and is not listening and does not hear your prayers. No, dear children, that is not the truth. When you are far from God, you cannot receive graces because you do not seek them with a firm faith. Day by day, I am praying for you, and I want to draw you ever more near to God, but I cannot if you don't want it. Therefore, dear children put your life in God's hands. I bless you all. Thank you for having responded to my call."

February 25, 1988

"Dear children! Today again I am calling you to prayer to complete surrender to God. You know that I love you and am coming here out of love so I could show you the path to peace and salvation for your souls. I want you to obey me and not permit Satan to seduce you. Dear children, Satan is very strong and, therefore, I ask you to dedicate your prayers to me so that those who are under his influence can be saved. Give witness by your life. Sacrifice your lives for the salvation of the world. I am with you, and I am grateful to you, but in heaven you shall receive the Father's reward which He has promised to you. Therefore, dear children, do not be afraid. If you pray, Satan cannot injure you even a little bit because you are God's children and He is watching over you. Pray and let the rosary always be in your hand as a sign to Satan that you belong to me. Thank you for having responded to my call."

March 25, 1988

"Dear children! Today also I am inviting you to a complete surrender to God. Dear children, you are not conscious of how God loves you with such a great love because He permits me to be with you so I can instruct you and help you to find the way of peace. This way, however, you cannot discover if you do not pray. Therefore, dear children, forsake everything and consecrate your time to God and God will bestow gifts upon you and bless you. Little children, don't forget that your life is fleeting like a spring flower which today is wondrously beautiful but tomorrow has vanished. Therefore, pray in such a way that your prayer, your surrender to God, may become like a road sign. That way, your witness will not only have value for yourselves but for all eternity. Thank you for having responded to my call."

April 25, 1988

"Dear children! God wants to make you holy. Therefore, through me He is inviting you to complete surrender. Let Holy Mass be your life. Understand that the church is God's palace, the place in which I gather you and want to show you the way to God. Come and pray. Neither look at others nor slander them, but rather, let your life be a testimony on the way of holiness. Churches deserve respect and are set apart as holy because God, who became man, dwells in them day and night. Therefore, little children, believe and pray that the Father increase your faith, and then ask for whatever you need. I am with you and I am rejoicing because of you conversion and I am protecting you with my motherly mantle. Thank you for having responded to my call."

May 25, 1988

"Dear children! I am inviting you to a complete surrender to God. Pray, little children, that Satan may not carry you about like the branches in the wind. Be strong in God. I desire that through you the whole world may get to know the God of joy. By your life bear witness for God's joy. Do not be anxious nor worried. God himself will help you and show you the way. I desire that you love all men with my love. Only in that way can love reign over the world. Little children, you are mine. I love you and want you to surrender to me so that I can lead you to God. Never cease praying so that Satan cannot take advantage of you. Pray for the knowledge that you are mine.

I bless you with blessings of joy. Thank you for having responded to my call."

June 25, 1988

"Dear children! I am calling you to that love which is loyal and pleasing to God. Little children, love bears everything bitter and difficult for the sake of Jesus who is love. Therefore, dear children, pray that God comes to your aid, not however according to your desire, but according to His love. Surrender yourself to God so that He may hear you, console you and forgive everything inside you which is a hindrance on the way of love. In this way God can move your life, and you will grow in love. Dear children, glorify God with a hymn of love so that God's love may be able to grow in you day by day to its fullness. Thank you for having responded to my call."

July 25, 1988

"Dear children! Today I am calling you to a complete surrender to God. Everything you do and everything you possess give over to God so that He can take control in your life as the King of all that you possess. That way, through me, God can lead you into the depths of the spiritual life. Little children, do not be afraid, because I am with you even if you think there is no way out and that Satan is in control. I am bringing peace to you I am your Mother, the Queen of Peace. I am blessing you with the blessings of joy so that for you God may be everything in your life. Thank you for having responded to my call."

August 25, 1988

"Dear children! Today I invite you all to rejoice in the life which God gives you. Little children, rejoice in God, the Creator, because He has created you so wonderfully. Pray that your life be joyful thanksgiving which flows out of your heart like a river of joy. Little children, give thanks unceasingly for all that you possess, for each little gift which God has given you, so that a joyful blessing always comes down from God upon your life. Thank you for having responded to my call."

September 25, 1988

"Dear children! Today I am inviting all of you, without exception, to the way of holiness in your life. God gave you the grace, the gift of holiness. Pray that you may, more and more, comprehend it, and in that way, you will be able, by your life, to bear witness for God. Dear children, I am blessing you and I intercede to God for you so that your way and your witness may be a complete one and a joy for God. Thank you for having responded to my call."

October 25, 1988

"Dear children! My invitation that you live the messages which I am giving you is a daily one, specially, little children, because I want to draw you closer to the Heart of Jesus. Therefore, little children, I am inviting you today to the prayer of consecration to Jesus, my dear Son, so that each of you may be His. And then I am inviting you to the consecration of my Immaculate Heart. I want you to consecrate yourselves as parents, as families and as parishioners so that all belong to God through my heart. Therefore, little children, pray that you comprehend the greatness of this message which I am giving you. I do not want anything for myself, rather all for the salvation of your soul. Satan is strong and therefore, you, little children, by constant prayer, press tightly against my motherly heart. Thank you for having responded to my call."

November 25, 1988

"Dear children! I call you to prayer, to have an encounter with God in prayer. God gives Himself to you, but He wants you to answer in your own freedom to his invitation. That is why little children during the day, find yourself a special time when you could pray in peace and humility, and have this meeting with God the creator. I am with you and I intercede for you in front of God, so watch in vigil, so that every encounter in prayer be the joy of your contact with God. Thank you for having responded to my call."

December 25, 1988

"Dear children! I call you to peace. Live it in your heart and all around you, so that all will know peace, peace that does not come from you but from God. Little children, today is a great day. Rejoice with me. Glorify the Nativity of Jesus through the peace that I give you. It is for this peace that I have come as your Mother, Queen of Peace. Today I give you my special blessing. Bring it to all creation, so that all creation will know peace. Thank you for having responded to my call."

1989

January 25, 1989

"Dear children! Today I am calling you to the way of holiness. Pray that you may comprehend the beauty and the greatness of this way where God reveals himself to you in a special way. Pray that you may be open to everything that God does through you that in your life you may be enabled to give thanks to God and to rejoice over everything that He does through each individual. I give you my blessing. Thank you for having responded to my call."

February 25, 1989

"Dear children! Today I invite you to prayer of the heart. Throughout this season of grace I wish each of you to be united with Jesus, but without unceasing prayer you cannot experience the beauty and greatness of the grace which God is offering you. Therefore, little children, at all times fill your heart with even the smallest prayers. I am with you and unceasingly keep watch over every heart which is given to me. Thank you for having responded to my call."

March 25, 1989

"Dear children! I am calling you to a complete surrender to God. I am calling you to great joy and peace which only God can give. I am with you and I intercede for you every day before God.

I call you, little children, to listen to me and to live the messages that I am giving you. Already for years you are invited to holiness but you are still far away. I am blessing you. Thank you for having responded to my call."

April 25, 1989

"Dear children! I am calling you to a complete surrender to God. Let everything that you possess be in the hands of God. Only in that way shall you have joy in your heart. Little children, rejoice in everything that you have. Give thanks to God because everything is God's gift to you. That way in your life you shall be able to give thanks for everything and discover God in everything even in the smallest flower. Thank you for having responded to my call."

May 25, 1989

"Dear children! I invite you now to be open to God. See, children, how nature is opening herself and is giving life and fruits. In the same way I invite you to live with God and to surrender completely to him. Children, I am with you and I want to introduce you continuously to the joy of life. I desire that everyone may discover the joy and love which can be found only in God and which only God can give. God doesn't want anything from you only your surrender. Therefore, children, decide seriously for God because everything else passes away. Only God doesn't pass away. Pray to be able to discover the greatness and joy of life which God gives you. Thank you for having responded to my call."

June 25, 1989

"Dear children! Today I am calling you to live the messages I have been giving you during the past eight years. This is the time of grace and I desire the grace of God be great for every single one of you. I am blessing you and I love you with a special love. Thank you for having responded to call."

July 25, 1989

"Dear children! Today I am calling you to renew your hearts. Open yourselves to God and surrender to him all your difficulties and crosses so God may turn everything into joy. Little children, you cannot open yourselves to God if you do not pray. Therefore, from today, decide to consecrate a time in the day only for an encounter with God in silence. In that way you will be able, with God, to witness my presence here. Little children, I do not wish to force you. Rather freely give God your time, like children of God. Thank you for having responded to my call."

August 25, 1989

"Dear children! I call you to prayer. By means of prayer, little children, you obtain joy and peace. Through prayer you are richer in the mercy of God. Therefore, little children, let prayer be the life of each one of you. Especially I call you to pray so that all those who are far away from God may be converted. Then our hearts shall be richer because God will rule in the hearts of all men. Therefore, little children, pray, pray, pray! Let prayers begin to rule in the whole world. Thank you for having responded to my call."

September 25, 1989

"Dear children! Today I invite you to give thanks to God for all the gifts you have discovered in the course of your life and even for the least gift that you have perceived. I give thanks with you and want all of you to experience the joy of these gifts. And I want God to be everything for each one of you. And then, little children, you can grow continuously on the way of holiness. Thank you for responding to my call."

October 25, 1989

"Dear children! Today also I am inviting you to prayer. I am always inviting you, but you are still far away. Therefore, from today, decide seriously to dedicate time to God. I am with you and I wish to teach you to pray with the heart. In prayer with the heart you shall encounter God. Therefore, little children, pray, pray, pray! Thank you for having responded to my call."

November 25, 1989

"Dear children! I am inviting you for years by these messages which I am giving you. Little children, by means of the messages I wish to make a very beautiful mosaic in your hearts, so I may be able to present each one of you to God like the original image. Therefore, little children, I desire that your decisions be free before God, because He has given you freedom. Therefore pray, so that, free from any influence of Satan, we may decide only for God. I am praying for you before God and I am seeking your surrender to God. Thank you for responding to my call."

December 25, 1989

"Dear children! Today I bless you in a special way with my motherly blessing and I am interceding for you before God that He gives you the gift of conversion of the heart. For years I am calling you and exhorting you to a deep spiritual life in simplicity, but you are so cold. Therefore, little children, I ask you to accept and live the messages with seriousness, so that your soul will not be sad when I will no longer be with you, and when I will no longer lead you like insecure children in their first steps. Therefore, little children, every day read the messages that I have given you and transform them into life. I love you and therefore I am calling you all to the way of salvation with God. Thank you for having responded to my call."

1990

January 25, 1990

"Dear children! Today I invite you to decide for God once again and to choose Him before everything and above everything, so that He may work miracles in your life and that day by day your life may become joy with Him. Therefore, little children, pray and do not permit Satan to work in your life through misunderstandings, the non-understanding and non-acceptance of one another. Pray that you may be able to comprehend the greatness and the beauty of the gift of life. Thank you for having responded to my call."

February 25, 1990

"Dear children! I invite you to surrender to God. In this season I specially want you to renounce all the things to which you are attached but which are hurting your spiritual life. Therefore, little children, decide completely for God, and do not allow Satan to come into your life through those things that hurt both you and your spiritual life. Little children, God is offering Himself to you in fullness, and you can discover and recognize Him only in prayer. Therefore make a decision for prayer. Thank you for having responded to call."

March 25, 1990

"Dear children! I am with you even if you are not conscious of it. I want to protect you from everything that Satan offers you and through which he wants to destroy you. As I bore Jesus in my womb, so also, dear children, do I wish to bear you into holiness. God wants to save you and sends you messages through men, nature, and so many things which can only help you to understand that you must change the direction of your life. Therefore, little children, understand also the greatness of the gift which God is giving you through me, so that I may protect you with my mantle and lead you to the joy of life. Thank you for having responded to my call."

April 25, 1990

"Dear children! Today I invite you to accept with seriousness and to live the messages which I am giving you. I am with you and I desire, dear children, that each one of you be ever closer to my heart. Therefore, little children, pray and seek the will of God in your everyday life. I desire that each one of you discover the way of holiness and grow in it until eternity. I will pray for you and intercede for you before God that you understand the greatness of this gift which God is giving me that I can be with you. Thank you for having responded to my call."

May 25, 1990

"Dear children! I invite you to decide with seriousness to live this novena. Consecrate the time to prayer and to sacrifice. I am with you and I desire to help you to grow in renunciation and mortification, that you may be able to understand the beauty of the life of people who go on giving themselves to me in [a] special way. Dear children, God blesses you day after day and desires a change of your life. Therefore, pray that you may have the strength to change your life. Thank you for having responded to my call."

June 25, 1990

"Dear children! Today I desire to thank you for all your sacrifices and for all your prayers. I am blessing you with my special motherly blessing. I invite you all to decide for God, so that from day to day you will discover His will in prayer. I desire, dear children, to call all of you to a full conversion so that joy will be in your hearts. I am happy that you are here today in such great numbers. Thank you for having responded to my call."

July 25, 1990

"Dear children! Today I invite you to peace. I have come here as the Queen of Peace and I desire to enrich you with my motherly peace. Dear children, I love you and I desire to bring all of you to the peace which only God gives and which enriches every heart. I invite you to become carriers and witnesses of my peace to this unpeaceful world. Let peace reign in the whole world which is without peace and longs for peace. I bless you with my motherly blessing. Thank you for having responded to my call."

August 25, 1990

"Dear children! I desire to invite you to take with seriousness and put into practice the messages which I am giving you. You know, little children, that I am with you and I desire to lead you along the same path to heaven, which is beautiful for those who discover it in prayer. Therefore, little children, do not forget that those messages which I am giving you have to be put into your everyday life in order that you might be able to say: "There, I have taken the messages and tried to live them." Dear children, I am protecting you before the heavenly Father by my own prayers. Thank you for having responded to my call."

September 25, 1990

"Dear children! I invite you to pray with the heart in order that your prayer may be a conversation with God. I desire each one of you to dedicate more time to God. Satan is strong and wants to destroy and deceive you in many ways.

Therefore, dear children, pray every day that your life will be good for yourselves and for all those you meet. I am with you and I am protecting you even though Satan wishes to destroy my plans and to hinder the desires which the Heavenly Father wants to realize here. Thank you for having responded to my call."

October 25, 1990

"Dear children! Today I call you to pray in a special way that you offer up sacrifices and good deeds for peace in the world. Satan is strong and with all his strength, desires to destroy the peace which comes from God. Therefore, dear children, pray in a special way with me for peace. I am with you and I desire to help you with my prayers and I desire to guide you on the path of peace. I bless you with my motherly blessing. Do not forget to live the messages of peace. Thank you for having responded to my call."

November 25, 1990

"Dear children! Today I invite you to do works of mercy with love and out of love for me and for your and my brothers and sisters. Dear children, all that you do for others, do it with great joy and humility towards God. I am with you and day after day I offer your sacrifices and prayers to God for the salvation of the world. Thank you for having responded to my call."

December 25, 1990

"Dear children! Today I invite you in a special way to pray for peace. Dear children, without peace you cannot experience the birth of the little Jesus neither today nor in your daily lives. Therefore, pray the Lord of Peace that He may protect you with His mantle and that He may help you to comprehend the greatness and the importance of peace in your heart. In this way you shall be able to spread peace from your heart throughout the whole world. I am with you and I intercede for you before God. Pray, because Satan wants to destroy my plans of peace. Be reconciled with one another and by means of your lives help peace reign in the whole earth. Thank you for having responded to my call."

1991

January 25, 1991

"Dear children! Today, like never before, I invite you to prayer. Let your prayer be a prayer for peace. Satan is strong and desires to destroy not only human life, but also nature and the planet on which you live. Therefore, dear children, pray that through prayer you can protect yourselves with God's blessing of peace. God has sent me among you so that I may help you. If you so wish, grasp for the rosary. Even the rosary alone can work miracles in the world and in your lives. I bless you and I remain with you for as long as it is God's will. Thank you for not betraying my presence here and I thank you because your response is serving the good and the peace."

February 25, 1991

"Dear children! Today, I invite you to decide for God, because distance from God is the fruit of the lack of peace in your hearts. God is only peace. Therefore, approach Him through your personal prayer and then live peace in your hearts and in this way peace will flow from your hearts like a river into the whole world. Do not talk about peace, but make peace. I am blessing each of you and each good decision of yours. Thank you for having responded to my call."

March 25, 1991

"Dear children! Again today I invite you to live the passion of Jesus in prayer, and in union with Him. Decide to give more time to God who gave you these days of grace. Therefore, dear children, pray and in a special way renew the love for Jesus for in your hearts. I am with you and I accompany you with my blessing any my prayers. Thank you for having responded to my call."

April 25, 1991

"Dear children! Today I invite you all so that your prayer be prayer with the heart. Let each of you find time for prayer so that in prayer you discover God. I do not desire you to talk about prayer, but to pray. Let your every day be filled with prayer of gratitude to God for life and for all that you have. I do not desire your life to pass by in words but that you glorify God with deeds. I am with you and I am grateful to God for every moment spent with you. Thank you for having responded to my call."

May 25, 1991

"Dear Children! Today I invite all of you who have heard my message of peace to realize it with seriousness and with love in your life. There are many who think that they are doing a lot by talking about the messages, but do not live them. Dear children, I invite you to life and to change all the negative in you, so that it all turns into the positive and life. Dear children, I am with you and I desire to help each of you to live and by living, to witness the good news. I am here, dear children, to help you and to lead you to heaven, and in heaven is the joy through which you can already live heaven now. Thank you for having responded to my call!"

June 25, 1991

"Dear children! Today on this great day which you have given to me, I desire to bless all of you and to say: these days while I am with you are days of grace. I desire to teach you and help you to walk the way of holiness. There are many people who do not desire to understand my messages and to accept with seriousness what I am saying. But you I therefore call and ask that by your lives and by your daily living you witness my presence. If you pray, God will help you to discover the true reason for my coming. Therefore, little children, pray and read the Sacred Scriptures so that through my coming you discover the message in Sacred Scripture for you. Thank you for having responded to my call."

July 25, 1991

"Dear Children! Today I invite you to pray for peace. At this time peace is being threatened in a special way, and I am seeking from you to renew fasting and prayer in your families. Dear children, I desire you to grasp the seriousness of the situation and that much of what will happen depends on your prayers and you are praying a little bit. Dear children, I am with you and I am inviting you to begin to pray and fast seriously as in the first days of my coming. Thank you for having responded to my call."

August 25, 1991

"Dear Children! Today also I invite you to prayer, now as never before when my plan has begun to be realised. Satan is strong and wants to sweep away plans of peace and joy and make you think that my Son is not strong in his decisions. Therefore, I call all of you, dear children to pray and fast still more firmly. I invite you to realize through the secrets I began in Fatima may be fulfilled. I call you, dear children, to grasp the importance of my coming and the seriousness of the situation. I want to save all souls and present them to God. Therefore, let us pray that everything I have begun be fully realised. Thank you for having responded to my call."

September 25, 1991

"Dear children! Today in a special way I invite you all to prayer and renunciation. For now as never before Satan wants to show the world his shameful face by which he wants to seduce as many people as possible onto the way of death and sin. Therefore, dear children, help my Immaculate Heart to triumph in the sinful world. I beseech all of you to offer prayers and sacrifices for my intentions so I can present them to God for what is most necessary. Forget your desires, dear children, and pray for what God desires, and not for what you desire. Thank you for having responded to my call."

October 25, 1991

"Dear children! Pray! Pray! Pray!"

November 25, 1991

"Dear Children! This time also I am inviting you to prayer. Pray that you might be able to comprehend what God desires to tell you through my presence and through the messages I am giving you. I desire to draw you ever closer to Jesus and to His wounded heart that you might be able to comprehend the immeasurable love which gave itself for each one of you. Therefore, dear children, pray that from your heart would flow a fountain of love to every person both to the one who hates you and to the one who despises you. That way you will be able through Jesus' love to overcome all the misery in this world of sorrows, which is without hope for those who do not know Jesus. I am with you and I love you with the immeasurable love of Jesus. Thank you for all your sacrifices and prayers. Pray so I might be able to help you still more. Your prayers are necessary to me. Thank you for having responded to my call."

December 25, 1991

"Dear children! Today in a special way I bring the little Jesus to you, that He may bless you with His blessing of peace and love. Dear children, do not forget that this is a grace which many people neither understand nor accept. Therefore, you who have said that you are mine, and seek my help, give all of yourself. First of all, give your love and example in your families. You say that Christmas is a family feast. Therefore, dear children, put God in the first place in your families, so that He may give you peace and may protect you not only from war, but also in peace protect you from every satanic attack. When God is with you, you have everything. But when you do not want Him, then you are miserable and lost, and you do not know on whose side you are. Therefore, dear children, decide for God. Then you will get everything. Thank you for having responded to my call."

1992

January 25, 1992

"Dear Children! Today, I am inviting you to a renewal of prayer in your families so that way every family will become a joy to my son Jesus. Therefore, dear children, pray and seek more time for Jesus and then you will be able to understand and accept everything, even the most difficult sicknesses and crosses. I am with you and I desire to take you into my heart and protect you, but you have not yet decided. Therefore, dear children, I am seeking for you to pray, so through prayer you would allow me to help you. Pray, my dear little children, so prayer becomes your daily bread. Thank you for having responded to my call."

February 25, 1992

"Dear children! Today I invite you to draw still closer to God through prayer. Only that way will I be able to help you and to protect you from every attack of Satan. I am with you and I intercede for you with God, that He protect you. But I need your prayers and your - "Yes." You get lost easily in material and human things, and forget that God is your greatest friend. Therefore, my dear little children, draw close to God so He may protect you and guard you from every evil. Thank you for having responded to my call!"

March 25, 1992

"Dear children! Today as never before I invite you to live my messages and to put them into practice in your life. I have come to you to help you and, therefore, I invite you to change your life because you have taken a path of misery, a path of ruin. When I told you: convert, pray, fast, be reconciled, you took these messages superficially. You started to live them and then you stopped, because it was difficult for you. No, dear children, when something is good, you have to persevere in the good and not think: God does not see me, He is not listening, He is not helping. And so you have gone away from God and from me because of your miserable interest. I wanted to create of you an oasis of peace, love and goodness. God wanted you, with your love and with His help, to do miracles and, thus, give an example. Therefore, here is what I say to you: Satan is playing with you and with your souls and I cannot help you because you are far away from my heart. Therefore, pray, live my messages and then you will see the miracles of God's love in your everyday life. Thank you for having responded to my call."

April 25, 1992

"Dear children! Today also I invite you to prayer. Only by prayer and fasting can war be stopped. Therefore, my dear little children, pray and by your life give witness that you are mine and that you belong to me, because Satan wishes in these turbulent days to seduce as many souls as possible. Therefore, I invite you to decide for God and He will protect you and show you what you should do and which path to take. I invite all those who have said "yes" to me to renew their consecration to my Son Jesus and to His Heart and to me so we can take you more intensely as instruments of peace in this unpeaceful world. Medjugorje is a sign to all of you and a call to pray and live the days of grace that God is giving you. Therefore, dear children, accept the call to prayer with seriousness. I am with you and your suffering is also mine. Thank you for having responded to my call."

May 25, 1992

"Dear children! Today also I invite you to prayer, so that through prayer you come still nearer to God. I am with you and I desire to lead you on the path to salvation that Jesus gives you. From day to day, I am nearer to you although you are not aware of it and you do not want to admit that you are only linked to me in a small way with your few prayers. When trials and problems arise, you say, "O God! O Mother! Where are you?" As for me, I only wait for your "Yes" to present to Jesus for Him to fill you with His grace. That is why, once more, please accept my call and start to pray in a new way until prayer becomes joy to you. Then you will discover that God is all-powerful in your daily life. I am with you and I am waiting for you. Thank you for having responded to my call."

June 25, 1992

"Dear children! Today I am happy, even if in my heart there is still a little sadness for all those who have started on this path and then have left it. My presence here is to take you on a new path, the path to salvation. This is why I call you, day after day to conversion. But if you do not pray, you cannot say that you are on the way to being converted. I pray for you and I intercede to God for peace; first peace in your hearts and also peace around you, so that God may be your peace. Thank you for having responded to my call."

July 25, 1992

"Dear children! Today also I invite you to prayer, a prayer of joy so that in these sad days no one amongst you may feel sadness in prayer, but a joyful meeting with God His Creator. Pray, little children, to be able to come closer to me and to feel through prayer what it is I desire from you. I am with you and each day I bless you with my maternal blessing so that Our Lord may fill you abundantly with His grace for your daily life. Give thanks to God for the grace of my being able to be with you because I assure you it is a great grace. Thank you for having responded to my call."

August 25, 1992

"Dear children! Today I desire to tell you that I love you. I love you with my maternal love and I invite you to open yourselves completely to me so that, through each one of you, I can convert and save this world which is full of sin and bad things. That is why, my dear little children, you should open yourselves completely to me so that I may carry you always further toward the marvelous love of God the Creator who reveals Himself to you from day to day. I am with you and I wish to reveal to you and show you the God who loves you. Thank you for having responded to my call."

September 25, 1992

"Dear children! Today again I would like to say to you that I am with you also in these troubled days during which Satan wishes to destroy all that my Son Jesus and I are building. He desires especially to destroy your souls. He wants to take you away as far as possible from the Christian life and from the commandments that the Church calls you to live. Satan wishes to destroy everything that is holy in you and around you. This is why, little children, pray, pray, pray to be able to grasp all that God is giving you through my coming. Thank you for having responded to my call."

October 25, 1992

"Dear children! I invite you to prayer now when Satan is strong and wishes to make as many souls as possible his own. Pray, dear children, and have more trust in me because I am here in order to help you and to guide you on a new path toward a new life. Therefore, dear little children, listen and live what I tell you because it is important for you when I shall not be with you any longer that you remember my words and all that I told you. I call you to begin to change your life from the beginning and that you decide for conversion not with words but with your life. Thank you for having responded to my call."

November 25, 1992

"Dear Children! Today, more than ever, I am calling you to pray. May your life become a continuous prayer. Without love you cannot pray. That is why I am calling you to love God, the Creator of your lives, above everything else. Then you will come to know God and will love Him in everything as He loves you. Dear children, it is a grace that I am with you. That is why you should accept and live my messages for your own good. I love you and that is why I am with you, in order to teach you and to lead you to a new life of conversion and renunciation. Only in this way will you discover God and all that which now seems so far away from you. Therefore, my dear children, pray. Thank you for having responded to my call."

December 25, 1992

"Dear children! I desire to place all of you under my mantle and protect you from all satanic attacks. Today is a day of peace, but in the whole world there is a great lack of peace. That is why I call you all to build a new world of peace with me through prayer. This I cannot do without you, and this is why I call all of you with my motherly love and God will do the rest. So, open yourselves to God's plan and to His designs to be able to cooperate with Him for peace and for everything that is good. Do not forget that your life does not belong to you, but is a gift with which you must bring joy to others and lead them to eternal life. May the tenderness of the little Jesus always accompany you. Thank you for having responded to my call."

Ivanka Ivanković-Elez was born on June 21, 1966 in Bijakovići, in the parish of Medjugorje. She has had daily apparitions from June 24, 1981 to May 7, 1985. On that last day, Our Lady entrusted the last of the ten secrets to her. Our Lady then told her that She would appear to her once a year on the anniversary of the Apparitions, on the 25th of each June, for the rest of her life. This is how it has been. Our Lady has asked her to pray especially for families.

Mirjana Dragičević-Soldo was born on March 18, 1965 in Sarajevo. She has had daily apparitions from June 24, 1981 to December 25, 1982. On that last day, Our Lady told her that She will continue to appear to her once a year on the 18th of March throughout her life. From 1983 until today, this is how it has been. Also, on the second of each month, Mirjana hears Our Lady's voice in her heart and prays with Our Lady for unbelievers. Sometimes, on the second of the month, she also sees Our Lady. Our Lady has entrusted the 10 secrets to her. She has been given the special ministry to pray for unbelievers, those who do not yet the love of God.

Vicka Ivanković was born on September 3, 1964 in Bijakovići. Our Lady first appeared to her on June 24, 1981. She continues to see Our Lady every day. So far, Our Lady has entrusted nine secrets to her. Our Lady has asked her to pray especially for the sick.

Marija Pavlović-Lunetti was born on April 1, 1965 in Bijakovići. Our Lady first appeared to her on June 25, 1981. She continues to have daily apparitions. Through Marija, Our Lady gives her message to the world on every 25th of the month. Up to now, Our Lady has entrusted nine secrets to her.
Our Lady has asked her to pray especially for the souls in Purgatory.

Ivan Dragičević was born on May 25, 1965 in Bijakovići. Since June 24, 1981, Our Lady has been appearing to him daily. Our Lady has entrusted nine secrets to him. Our Lady has asked him to pray especially for priests and the youth.

Jakov Čolo was born on March 6, 1971 in Bijakovići. He has daily apparitions since June 25, 1981. Our Lady appeared to Jakov for the last time on September 12, 1998 and confided the tenth secret to him. She also told him that she would appear to him each year on the feast of the  birth of her Son. Jakov lives in the Parish of Medjugorje. Our lady has asked him to pray especially for priests.

St. James' Church in 1984

"...What I want from you is to show me your love by coming to Mass, and the Lord will reward you abundantly. ..." (21-11-1985)

St. James' Church now

"..By living Holy Mass each day, you will feel the need for holiness and you will grow in holiness. I am close to you and intercede before God for each you, so that he may give you strength to change your heart. .."

(25-1-1998)

107

Old Photo of Visionaries – " ... Today also I am calling you to prayer. Your prayers are necessary to me so that

New photo of Visionaries - " ... This Lent is a special incentive for you to change. Start from this moment. Turn off the television and renounce various things that are of no value. ... " (13-2-1986)

The Risen Christ, Easter 2011
"May this time be a time of personal prayer for you, so that the
seed of faith may grow in your hearts" (25th January, 2010)

Visionary Marija prays on Apparition Hill, 1984.
" ... I am with you and I wish to teach you to pray with the
heart. In prayer with the heart you shall encounter God..."
(25th October, 1989)

111

Blue Cross area where Mirjana usually receives a mesage from Our Lady on the 2nd od every month.

"Open your hearts, little children and let your hands be extended and generous, so that, through you, every

Križevac today - "...pray at the foot of the Cross for peace..." (6-9-84)

Road from Križevac to church, March 1984

Locals greeting pilgrim children outside Vicka's house, 1984.

"Dear children, encourage the very young to prayer, and the young to go to Holy Mass. ..." (7-3-1985)

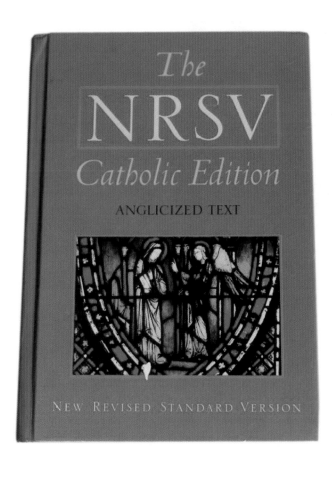

"Every family must pray family prayer and read the bible." (14-2-1985)

"Dear children! Today I call you to read the Bible every day in your homes and let it be in a visible place so as always to encourage you to read it and pray. ..." (18-10-1984)

Fasting

"Dear children! Today I call you to renew prayer and fasting with even greater enthusiasm until prayer becomes a joy for you. Little children, the one who prays is not afraid of the future and he one who fasts is not afraid of evil. Once again, I repeat to you: only through prayer and fasting also wars can be stopped – wars of your unbelief and fear for the future. I am with you and am teaching you little children: your peace and hope are in God. That is why draw closer to God and put Him in the first place in your life. Thank you for having responded to my call."

(25-1-2001)

1993

January 25, 1993

"Dear children! Today I call you to accept and live my messages with seriousness. These days are the days when you need to decide for God, for peace and for the good. May every hatred and jealousy disappear from your life and your thoughts, and may there only dwell love for God and for your neighbour. Thus, and only thus shall you be able to discern the signs of the time. I am with you and I guide you into a new time, a time which God gives you as grace so that you may get to know him more. Thank you for having responded to my call."

February 25, 1993

"Dear children! Today I bless you with my motherly blessing and I invite you all to conversion. I wish that each of you decide for a change of life and that each of you works more in the Church not through words and thoughts but through example, so that your life may be a joyful testimony for Jesus. You cannot say that you are converted, because your life must become a daily conversion. In order to understand what you have to do, little children, pray and God will give you what you completely have to do, and where you have to change. I am with you and place you all under my mantle. Thank you for having responded to my call."

March 25, 1993

"Dear children! Today like never I call you to pray for peace, for peace in your hearts, peace in your families and peace in the whole world, because Satan wants war, wants lack of peace, wants to destroy all which is good. Therefore, dear children, pray, pray, pray. Thank you for having responded to my call."

April 25, 1993

"Dear children! Today I invite you all to awaken your hearts to love. Go into nature and look how nature is awakening and it will be a help to you to open your hearts to the love of God, the Creator. I desire you to awaken love in your families so that where there is unrest and hatred, love will reign and when there is love in your hearts then there is also prayer. And, dear children, do not forget that I am with you and I am helping you with my prayer that God may give you the strength to love. I bless and love you with my motherly love. Thank you for having responded to my call."

May 25, 1993

"Dear children! Today I invite you to open yourselves to God by means of prayer so the Holy Spirit may begin to work miracles in you and through you. I am with you and I intercede before God for each one of you because, dear children, each one of you is important in my plan of salvation. I invite you to be carriers of good and peace. God can give you peace only if you convert and pray. Therefore, my dear little children, pray, pray, pray and do that which the Holy Spirit inspires you. Thank you for having responded to my call."

June 25, 1993

"Dear children! Today I also rejoice at your presence here. I bless you with my motherly blessing and intercede for each one of you before God. I call you anew to live my messages and to put them into life and practice. I am with you and bless all of you day by day. Dear children, these are special times and, therefore, I am with you to love and protect you; to protect your hearts from Satan and to bring you all closer to the heart of my Son, Jesus. Thank you for having responded to my call."

July 25, 1993

"Dear children! I thank you for your prayers and for the love you show towards me. I invite you to decide to pray for my intentions. Dear children, offer novenas, making sacrifices wherein you feel the most bound. I want your life to be bound to me. I am your Mother, little children, and I do not want Satan to deceive you for He wants to lead you the wrong way, but he cannot if you do not permit him. Therefore, little children, renew prayer in your hearts, and then you will understand my call and my live desire to help you. Thank you for having responded to my call."

August 25, 1993

"Dear children! I want you to understand that I am your Mother, that I want to help you and call you to prayer. Only by prayer can you understand and accept my messages and practice them in your life. Read Sacred Scripture, live it, and pray to understand the signs of the times.

This is a special time, therefore, I am with you to draw you close to my heart and the heart of my Son, Jesus. Dear little children, I want you to be children of the light and not of the darkness. Therefore, live what I am telling you. Thank you for having responded to my call."

September 25, 1993

"Dear children! I am your Mother and I invite you to come closer to God through prayer because only He is your peace, your Saviour. Therefore, little children, do not seek comfort in material things, but rather seek God. I am praying for you and I intercede before God for each individual. I am looking for your prayers that you accept me and accept my messages as in the first days of the apparitions and only then when you open your hearts and pray will miracles happen. Thank you for having responded to my call."

October 25, 1993

"Dear children! These years I have been calling you to pray, to live what I am telling you, but you are living my messages a little. You talk, but do not live, that is why little children, this war is lasting so long. I invite you to open yourselves to God and in your hearts to live with God, living the good and giving witness to my messages. I love you and wish to protect you from every evil, but you do not desire it. Dear children, I cannot help you if you do not live God's commandments, if you do not live the Mass, if you do not give up sin. I invite you to be apostles of love and goodness. In this world of unrest give witness to God and

God's love, and God will bless you and give you what you seek from Him. Thank you for having responded to my call."

November 25, 1993

"Dear children! I invite you in this time like never before to prepare for the coming of Jesus. Let little Jesus reign in your hearts and only then when Jesus is your friend will you be happy. It will not be difficult for you either to pray or offer sacrifices or to witness Jesus' greatness in your life because He will give you strength and joy in this time. I am close to you by my intercession and prayer and I love and bless all of you. Thank you for having responded to my call."

December 25, 1993

"Dear children! Today I rejoice with the little Jesus and I desire that Jesus' joy may enter into every heart. Little children, with the message I give you a blessing with my son Jesus, so that in every heart peace may reign. I love you, little children, and I invite all of you to come closer to me by means of prayer. You talk and talk but do not pray. Therefore, little children, decide for prayer. Only in this way will you be happy and God will give your what you seek from Him. Thank you for having responded to my call."

1994

January 25, 1994

"Dear children! You are all my children. I love you. But, little children, you must not forget that without prayer you cannot be close to me. In these times Satan wants to create disorder in your hearts and in your families. Little children, do not give in. You should not allow him to lead you and your life. I love you and intercede before God for you. Little children, pray. Thank you for having responded to my call."

February 25, 1994

"Dear children! Today I thank you for your prayers. All of you have helped me so that this war may end as soon as possible. I am close to you and I pray for each one of you and I beg you: pray, pray, pray. Only through prayer can we defeat evil and protect all that Satan wants to destroy in your lives. I am your Mother and I love you all equally, and I intercede for you before God. Thank you for having responded to my call."

March 25, 1994

"Dear children! Today I rejoice with you and I invite you to open yourselves to me, and become an instrument in my hands for the salvation of the world. I desire, little children, that all of you who have felt the odour of holiness through these messages which I am giving you to carry, to carry it into this world, hungry for God and God's love. I thank you all for having responded in such a number and I bless you all with my motherly blessing. Thank you for having responded to my call."

April 25, 1994

"Dear children! Today I invite you to decide to pray according to my intention. Little children, I invite each one of you to help my plan to be realised through this parish. Now I invite you in a special way, little children, to decide to go along the way of holiness. Only this way will you be close to me. I love you and I desire to conduct you all with me to Paradise. But, if you do not pray and if you are not humble and obedient to the messages which I am giving you, I cannot help you. Thank you for having responded to my call."

May 25, 1994

"Dear children! I invite you all to have more trust in me and to live my messages more deeply. I am with you and I intercede before God for you but also I wait for your hearts to open up to my messages. Rejoice because God loves you and gives you the possibility to convert every day and to believe more in God the Creator. Thank you having responded to my call."

June 25, 1994

"Dear children! Today I rejoice in my heart in seeing you all present here. I bless you and I call you all to decide to live my messages which I give you here. I desire, little children, to guide you all to Jesus because He is your salvation. Therefore, little children, the more you pray the more you will be mine and of my Son, Jesus. I bless you all with my motherly blessing and I thank you for having responded to my call."

July 25, 1994

"Dear children! Today I invite you to decide to give time patiently for prayer. Little children, you cannot say you are mine and that you have experienced conversion through my messages if you are not ready to give time to God every day. I am close to you and I bless you all. Little children, do not forget that if you do not pray you are not close to me, nor are you close to the Holy Spirit who leads you along the path to holiness. Thank you for having responded to my call."

August 25, 1994

"Dear children! Today I am united with you in prayer in a special way, praying for the gift of the presence of my most beloved son in your home country. Pray, little children, for the health of my most beloved son, who suffers, and whom I have chosen for these times. I pray and intercede before my Son, Jesus, so that the dream that your fathers had may be fulfilled. Pray, little children, in a special way, because Satan is strong and wants to destroy hope in your heart. I bless you. Thank you for having responded to my call."

September 25, 1994

"Dear children! I rejoice with you and I invite you to prayer. Little children, pray for my intention. Your prayers are necessary to me, through which I desire to bring you closer to God. He is your salvation. God sends me to help you and to guide you towards paradise, which is your goal. Therefore, little children, pray, pray, pray. Thank you for having responded to my call."

October 25, 1994

"Dear children! I am with you and I rejoice today because the Most High has granted me to be with you and to teach you and to guide you on the path of perfection. Little children, I wish you to be a beautiful bouquet of flowers which I wish to present to God for the day of All Saints. I invite you to open yourselves and to live, taking the saints as an example. Mother Church has chosen them, that they may be an impulse for your daily life. Thank you for having responded to my call!"

November 25, 1994

"Dear children! Today I call you to prayer. I am with you and I love you all. I am your Mother and I wish that your hearts be similar to my heart. Little children, without prayer you cannot live and say that you are mine. Prayer is joy. Prayer is what the human heart desires. Therefore, get closer, little children, to my Immaculate Heart and you will discover God. Thank you for having responded to my call."

December 25, 1994

"Dear children! Today I rejoice with you and I am praying with you for peace: peace in your hearts, peace in your families, peace in your desires, peace in the whole world. May the King of Peace bless you today and give you peace. I bless you and I carry each one of you in my heart. Thank you for having responded to my call."

1995

January 25, 1995

"Dear children! I invite you to open the door of your heart to Jesus as the flower opens itself to the sun. Jesus desires to fill your hearts with peace and joy. You cannot, little children, realise peace if you are not at peace with Jesus. Therefore, I invite you to Confession so Jesus may be your truth and peace. So, little children, pray to have the strength to realise what I am telling you. I am with you and I love you. Thank you for having responded to my call."

February 25, 1995

"Dear children! Today I invite you to become missionaries of my messages, which I am giving here through this place that is dear to me. God has allowed me to stay this long with you and therefore, little children, I invite you to live with love the messages I give and to transmit them to the whole world, so that a river of love flows to people who are full of hatred and without peace. I invite you, little children, to become peace where there is no peace and light where there is darkness, so that each heart accepts the light and the way of salvation. Thank you for having responded to my call."

March 25, 1995

"Dear Children! Today I invite you to live the peace in your hearts and families. There is no peace, little children, where there is no prayer and there is no love, where there is no faith. Therefore, little children, I invite you all, to decide again today for conversion. I am close to you and I invite you all, little children, into my embrace to help you, but you do not want [it] and in this way, Satan is tempting you, and in the smallest thing, your faith disappears. This is why little children, pray and through prayer, you will have blessing and peace. Thank you for having responded to my call."

April 25, 1995

"Dear children! Today I call you to love. Little children, without love you can neither live with God nor with brother. Therefore, I call all of you to open your hearts to the love of God that is so great and open to each one of you. God, out of love for man, has sent me among you to show you the path of salvation, the path of love. If you do not first love God, then you will neither be able to love neighbour nor the one you hate. Therefore, little children, pray and through prayer you will discover love. Thank you for having responded to my call."

May 25, 1995

"Dear Children! I invite you, little children, to help me through your prayers so that as many hearts as possible come close to my Immaculate Heart. Satan is strong and with all his forces wants to bring closer the most people possible to himself and to sin. That is why he is on the prowl to snatch more every moment. I beg you, little children, pray and help me to help you. I am your mother and I love you and that is why I wish to help you. Thank you for having responded to my call."

June 25, 1995

"Dear Children! Today I am happy to see you in such great numbers, that you have responded and have come to live my messages. I invite you, little children, to be my joyful carriers of peace in this troubled world. Pray for peace so that as soon as possible a time of peace, which my heart waits impatiently for, may reign. I am near to you, little children, and intercede for every one of you before the Most High. I bless you with my motherly blessing. Thank you for having responded to my call."

July 25, 1995

"Dear children! Today I invite you to prayer because only in prayer can you understand my coming here. The Holy Spirit will enlighten you to understand that you must convert. Little children, I wish to make of you a most beautiful bouquet prepared for eternity but you do not accept the way of conversion, the way of salvation that I am offering you through these apparitions. Little children, pray, convert your hearts and come closer to me. May good overcome evil. I love you and bless you. Thank you for having responded to my call."

August 25, 1995

"Dear children! Today I invite you to prayer. Let prayer be life for you. A family cannot say that it is in peace if it does not pray. Therefore, let your morning begin with morning prayer, and the evening end with thanksgiving. Little children, I am with you, and I love you and I bless you and I wish for every one of you to be in my embrace. You cannot be in my embrace if you are not ready to pray every day. Thank you for having responded to my call."

September 25, 1995

"Dear Children! Today I invite you to fall in love with the Most Holy Sacrament of the Altar. Adore Him, little children, in your Parishes and in this way you will be united with the entire world. Jesus will become your friend and you will not talk of Him like someone whom you barely know. Unity with Him will be a joy for you and you will become witnesses to the love of Jesus that He has for every creature. Little children, when you adore Jesus you are also close to me. Thank you for having responded to my call."

October 25, 1995

"Dear Children! Today I invite you to go into nature because there you will meet God the Creator. Today I invite you, little children, to thank God for all that He gives you. In thanking Him you will discover the Most High and all the goods that surround you. Little children, God is great and His love for every creature is great. Therefore, pray to be able to understand the love and goodness of God. In the goodness and the love of God the Creator, I also am with you as a gift. Thank you for having responded to my call."

November 25, 1995

"Dear Children! Today I invite you that each of you begin again to love, in the first place, God who saved and redeemed each of you, and then brothers and sisters in your proximity. Without love, little children, you cannot grow in holiness and cannot do good deeds. Therefore, little children, pray without ceasing that God reveals His love to you. I have invited all of you to unite yourselves with me and to love. Today I am with you and invite you to discover love in your hearts and in the families. For God to live in your hearts, you must love. Thank you for having responded to my call."

December 25, 1995

"Dear Children! Today I also rejoice with you and I bring you little Jesus, so that He may bless you. I invite you, dear children, so that your life may be united with Him. Jesus is the King of Peace and only He can give you the peace that you seek. I am with you and I present you to Jesus in a special way, now in this new time in which one should decide for Him. This time is the time of grace. Thank you for having responded to my call."

1996

January 25, 1996

"Dear Children! Today I invite you to decide for peace. Pray that God give[s] you the true peace. Live peace in your hearts and you will understand, dear children, that peace is the gift of God. Dear children, without love you cannot live peace. The fruit of peace is love and the fruit of love is forgiveness. I am with you and I invite all of you, little children, that before all else forgive in the family and then you will be able to forgive others. Thank you for having responded to my call."

February 25, 1996

"Dear children! Today I invite you to conversion. This is the most important message that I have given you here. Little children, I wish that each of you become a carrier of my messages. I invite you, little children, to live the messages that I have given you over these years. This time is a time of grace. Especially now, when the Church also is inviting you to prayer and conversion. I also, little children, invite you to live my messages that I have given you during the time since I appear here. Thank you for having responded to my call."

March 25, 1996

"Dear children! I invite you to decide again to love God above all else. In this time when due to the spirit of consumerism one forgets what it means to love and to cherish true values, I invite you again, little children, to put God in the first place in your life. Do not let Satan attract you through material things but, little children, decide for God who is freedom and love. Choose life and not death of the soul, little children, and in this time when you meditate upon the suffering and death of Jesus I invite you to decide for life which blossomed through the Resurrection, and that your life may be renewed today through conversion that shall lead you to eternal life. Thank you for having responded to my call."

April 25, 1996

"Dear children! Today I invite you again to put prayer in the first place in your families. Little children, when God is in the first place, then you will, in all that you do, seek the will of God. In this way your daily conversion will become easier. Little children, seek with humility that which is not in order in your hearts, and you shall understand what you have to do. Conversion will become a daily duty that you will do with joy. Little children, I am with you, I bless you all and I invite you to become my witnesses by prayer and personal conversion. Thank you for having responded to my call."

May 25, 1996

"Dear children! Today I wish to thank you for all your prayers and sacrifices that you, during this month which is consecrated to me, have offered to me. Little children, I also wish that you all become active during this time that is through me connected to heaven in a special way. Pray in order to understand that you all, through your life and your example, ought to collaborate in the work of salvation. Little children, I wish that all people convert and see me and my son, Jesus, in you. I will intercede for you and help you to become the light. In helping the other, your soul will also find salvation. Thank you for having responded to my call."

June 25, 1996

"Dear children! Today I thank you for all the sacrifices you have offered me these days. Little children, I invite you to open yourselves to me and to decide for conversion. Your hearts, little children, are still not completely open to me and therefore, I invite you again to open to prayer so that in prayer the Holy Spirit will help you, that your hearts become of flesh and not of stone. Little children, thank you for having responded to my call and for having decided to walk with me toward holiness."

July 25, 1996

"Dear children! Today I invite you to decide every day for God. Little children, you speak much about God, but you witness little with your life. Therefore, little children, decide for conversion, that your life may be true before God, so that in the truth of your life you witness the beauty God gave you. Little children, I invite you again to decide for prayer because through prayer, you will be able to live the conversion. Each one of you shall become in the simplicity, similar to a child which is open to the love of the Father. Thank you for having responded to my call."

August 25, 1996

"Dear children! Listen, because I wish to speak to you and to invite you to have more faith and trust in God, who loves you immeasurably. Little children, you do not know how to live in the grace of God, that is why I call you all anew, to carry the word of God in your heart and in thoughts. Little children, place the Sacred Scripture in a visible place in your family, and read and live it. Teach your children, because if you are not an example to them, children depart into godlessness. Reflect and pray and then God will be born in your heart and your heart will be joyous. Thank you for having for responded to my call."

September 25, 1996

"Dear children! Today I invite you to offer your crosses and suffering for my intentions. Little children, I am your mother and I wish to help you by seeking for you the grace from God. Little children, offer your sufferings as a gift to God so they become a most beautiful flower of joy. That is why, little children, pray that you may understand that suffering can become joy and the cross the way of joy. Thank you for having for responded to my call."

October 25, 1996

"Dear children! Today I invite you to open yourselves to God the Creator, so that He changes you. Little children, you are dear to me. I love you all and I call you to be closer to me and that your love towards my Immaculate Heart be more fervent. I wish to renew you and lead you with my Heart to the Heart of Jesus, which still today suffers for you and calls you to conversion and renewal. Through you, I wish to renew the world. Comprehend, little children, that you are today the salt of the earth and the light of the world. Little children, I invite you and I love you and in a special way implore: Convert!" Thank you for having responded to my call."

November 25, 1996

"Dear children! Today, again, I invite you to pray, so that through prayer, fasting and small sacrifices you may prepare yourselves for the coming of Jesus. May this time, little children, be a time of grace for you. Use every moment and do good, for only in this way will you feel the birth of Jesus in your hearts. If with your life you give an example and become a sign of God's love, joy will prevail in the hearts of men. Thank you for having responded to my call."

December 25, 1996

"Dear children! Today I am with you in a special way, holding little Jesus in my lap and I invite you, little children, to open yourselves to His call. He calls you to joy. Little children, joyfully live the messages of the Gospel, which I am repeating in the time since I am with you. Little children, I am your Mother and I desire to reveal to you the God of love and the God of peace. I do not desire for your life to be in sadness but that it be realised in joy for eternity, according to the Gospel. Only in this way will your life have meaning. Thank you for having responded to my call."

1997

January 25, 1997

"Dear children! I invite you to reflect about your future. You are creating a new world without God, only with your own strength and that is why you are unsatisfied and without joy in the heart. This time is my time and that is why, little children, I invite you again to pray. When you find unity with God, you will feel hunger for the word of God and your heart, little children, will overflow with joy. You will witness God's love wherever you are. I bless you and I repeat to you that I am with you to help you. Thank you for having responded to my call."

February 25, 1997

"Dear children! Today I invite you in a special way to open yourselves to God the Creator and to become active. I invite you, little children, to see at this time who needs your spiritual or material help. By your example, little children, you will be the extended hands of God, which humanity is seeking. Only in this way will you understand, that you are called to witness and to become joyful carriers of God's word and of His love. Thank you for having responded to my call."

March 25, 1997

"Dear children! Today, in a special way, I invite you to take the cross in the hands and to meditate on the wounds of Jesus. Ask of Jesus to heal your wounds, which you, dear children, during your life sustained because of your sins or the sins of your parents. Only in this way, dear children, you will understand that the world is in need of healing of faith in God the Creator. By Jesus' passion and death on the cross, you will understand that only through prayer you, too, can become true apostles of faith; when, in simplicity and prayer, you live faith which is a gift. Thank you for having responded to my call."

April 25, 1997

"Dear children! Today I call you to have your life be connected with God the Creator, because only in this way will your life have meaning and you will comprehend that God is love. God sends me to you out of love, that I may help you to comprehend that without Him there is no future or joy and, above all, there is no eternal salvation. Little children, I call you to leave sin and to accept prayer at all times, that you may in prayer come to know the meaning of your life. God gives Himself to him who seeks Him. Thank you for having responded to my call."

May 25, 1997

"Dear children! Today I invite you to glorify God and for the Name of God to be holy in your hearts and in your life. Little children, when you are in the holiness of God, He is with you and gives you peace and joy which come from God only through prayer. That is why, little children, renew prayer in your families and your heart will glorify the holy Name of God and heaven will reign in your heart. I am close to you and I intercede for you before God. Thank you for having responded to my call."

June 25, 1997

"Dear children! Today I am with you in a special way and I bring you my motherly blessing of peace. I pray for you and I intercede for you before God, so that you may comprehend that each of you is a carrier of peace. You cannot have peace if your heart is not at peace with God. That is why, little children, pray, pray, pray, because prayer is the foundation of your peace. Open your heart and give time to God so that He will be your friend. When true friendship with God is realised, no storm can destroy it. Thank you for having responded to my call."

July 25, 1997

"Dear children! Today I invite you to respond to my call to prayer. I desire, dear children, that during this time you find a corner for personal prayer. I desire to lead you towards prayer with the heart. Only in this way will you comprehend that your life is empty without prayer. You will discover the meaning of your life when you discover God in prayer. That is why, little children, open the door of your heart and you will comprehend that prayer is joy without which you cannot live. Thank you for having responded to my call."

August 25, 1997

"Dear children! God gives me this time as a gift to you, so that I may instruct and lead you on the path of salvation. Dear children, now you do not comprehend this grace, but soon a time will come when you will lament for these messages. That is why, little children, live all of the words which I have given you through this time of grace and renew prayer, until prayer becomes a joy for you. Especially, I call all those who have consecrated themselves to my Immaculate Heart to become an example to others. I call all priests and religious brothers and sisters to pray the rosary and to teach others to pray. The rosary, little children, is especially dear to me. Through the rosary open your heart to me and I am able to help you. Thank you for having responded to my call."

September 25, 1997

"Dear children! Today I call you to comprehend that without love you cannot comprehend that God needs to be in the first place in your life. That is why, little children, I call you all to love, not with a human but with God's love. In this way, your life will be more beautiful and without an interest. You will comprehend that God gives Himself to you in the simplest way out of love. Little children, so that you may comprehend my words which I give you out of love, pray, pray, pray and you will be able to accept others with love and to forgive all who have done evil to you. Respond with prayer; prayer is a fruit of love towards God the Creator. Thank you for having responded to my call."

October 25, 1997

"Dear children! Also today I am with you and I call all of you to renew yourselves by living my messages. Little children, may prayer be life for you and may you be an example to others. Little children, I desire for you to become carriers of peace and of God's joy to today's world without peace. That is why, little children, pray, pray, pray! I am with you and I bless you with my motherly peace. Thank you for having responded to my call."

November 25, 1997

"Dear children! Today I invite you to comprehend your Christian vocation. Little children, I led and am leading you through this time of grace, that you may become conscious of your Christian vocation. Holy martyrs died witnessing: I am a Christian and love God over everything. Little children, today also I invite you to rejoice and be joyful Christians, responsible and conscious that God called you in a special way to be joyfully extended hands toward those who do not believe, and that through the example of your life, they may receive faith and love for God. Therefore, pray, pray, pray that your heart may open and be sensitive for the Word of God. Thank you for having responded to my call."

December 25, 1997

"Dear children! Also today I rejoice with you and I call you to the good. I desire that each of you reflect and carry peace in your heart and say: I want to put God in the first place in my life. In this way, little children, each of you will become holy. Little children, tell everyone, I want the good for you and He will respond with the good and, little children, good will come to dwell in the heart of each man. Little children, tonight I bring to you the good of my Son who gave His life to save you. That is why, little children, rejoice and extend your hands to Jesus who is only good. Thank you for having responded to my call."

1998

January 25, 1998

"Dear children! Today again I call all of you to prayer. Only with prayer, dear children, will your heart change, become better, and be more sensitive to the Word of God. Little children, do not permit Satan to pull you apart and to do with you what he wants. I call you to be responsible and determined and to consecrate each day to God in prayer. May Holy Mass, little children, not be a habit for you, but life. By living Holy Mass each day, you will feel the need for holiness and you will grow in holiness. I am close to you and intercede before God for each of you, so that He may give you strength to change your heart. Thank you for having responded to my call."

February 25, 1998

"Dear children! Also today I am with you and I, again, call all of you to come closer to me through your prayers. In a special way, I call you to renunciation in this time of grace. Little children, meditate on and live, through your little sacrifices, the passion and death of Jesus for each of you. Only if you come closer to Jesus will you comprehend the immeasurable love He has for each of you. Through prayer and your renunciation you will become more open to the gift of faith and love towards the Church and the people who are around you. I love you and bless you. Thank you for having responded to my call."

March 25, 1998

"Dear children! Also today I call you to fasting and renunciation. Little children, renounce that which hinders you from being closer to Jesus. In a special way I call you: Pray, because only through prayer will you be able to overcome your will and discover the will of God even in the smallest things. By your daily life, little children, you will become an example and witness that you live for Jesus or against Him and His will. Little children, I desire that you become apostles of love. By loving, little children, it will be recognized that you are mine. Thank you for having responded to my call."

April 25, 1998

"Dear children! Today I call you, through prayer, to open yourselves to God as a flower opens itself to the rays of the morning sun. Little children, do not be afraid. I am with you and I intercede before God for each of you so that your heart receives the gift of conversion. Only in this way, little children, will you comprehend the importance of grace in these times and God will become nearer to you. Thank you for having responded to my call."

May 25, 1998

"Dear children! Today I call you, through prayer and sacrifice, to prepare yourselves for the coming of the Holy Spirit. Little children, this is a time of grace and so, again, I call you to decide for God the Creator. Allow Him to transform and change you. May your heart be prepared to listen to, and live, everything which the Holy Spirit has in His plan for each of you. Little children, allow the Holy Spirit to lead you on the way of truth and salvation towards eternal life. Thank you for having responded to my call."

June 25, 1998

"Dear children! Today I desire to thank you for living my messages. I bless you all with my motherly blessing and I bring you all before my Son Jesus. Thank you for having responded to my call."

July 25, 1998

"Dear children! Today, little children, I invite you, through prayer, to be with Jesus, so that through a personal experience of prayer you may be able to discover the beauty of God's creatures. You cannot speak or witness about prayer, if you do not pray. That is why, little children, in the silence of the heart, remain with Jesus, so that He may change and transform you with His love. This, little children, is a time of grace for you. Make good use of it for your personal conversion, because when you have God, you have everything. Thank you for having responded to my call."

August 25, 1998

"Dear children! Today I invite you to come still closer to me through prayer. Little children, I am your mother, I love you and I desire that each of you be saved and thus be with me in Heaven. That is why, little children, pray, pray, pray until your life becomes prayer. Thank you for having responded to my call."

September 25, 1998

"Dear children! Today, I call you to become my witnesses by living the faith of your fathers. Little children, you seek signs and messages and do not see that, with every morning sunrise, God calls you to convert and to return to the way of truth and salvation. You speak much, little children, but you work little on your conversion. That is why, convert and start to live my messages, not with your words but with your life. In this way, little children, you will have the strength to decide for the true conversion of the heart. Thank you for having responded to my call."

October 25, 1998

"Dear children! Today I call you to come closer to my Immaculate Heart. I call you to renew in your families the fervour of the first days when I called you to fasting, prayer and conversion. Little children, you accepted my messages with open hearts, although you did not know what prayer was. Today, I call you to open yourselves completely to me so that I may transform you and lead you to the heart of my son Jesus, so that He can fill you with His love. Only in this way, little children, will you find true peace - the peace that only God gives you. Thank you for having responded to my call."

November 25, 1998

"Dear children! Today I call you to prepare yourselves for the coming of Jesus. In a special way, prepare your hearts. May Holy Confession be the first act of conversion for you and then, dear children, decide for holiness. May your conversion and decision for holiness begin today and not tomorrow. Little children, I call you all to the way of salvation and I desire to show you the way to Heaven. That is why, little children, be mine and decide with me for holiness. Little children, accept prayer with seriousness and pray, pray, pray. Thank you for having responded to my call."

December 25, 1998

"Dear children! In this Christmas joy I desire to bless you with my blessing. In a special way, little children, I give you the blessing of little Jesus. May He fill you with His peace. Today, little children, you do not have peace and yet you yearn for it. That is why, with my Son Jesus, on this day I call you to pray, pray, pray, because without prayer you do not have joy or peace or a future. Yearn for peace and seek it, for God is true peace. Thank you for having responded to my call."

1999

January 25, 1999

"Dear children! I again invite you to prayer. You have no excuse to work more because nature still lies in deep sleep. Open yourselves in prayer. Renew prayer in your families. Put Holy Scripture in a visible place in your families, read it, reflect on it and learn how God loves His people. His love shows itself also in present times because He sends me to call you upon the path of salvation. Thank you for having responded to my call."

February 25, 1999

"Dear children! Also today I am with you in a special way contemplating and living the passion of Jesus in my heart. Little children, open your hearts and give me everything that is in them: joys, sorrows and each, even the smallest, pain, that I may offer them to Jesus; so that with His immeasurable love, He may burn and transform your sorrows into the joy of His resurrection. That is why, I now call you in a special way, little children, for your hearts to open to prayer, so that through prayer you may become friends of Jesus. Thank you for having responded to my call."

March 25, 1999

"Dear children! I call you to prayer with the heart. In a special way, little children, I call you to pray for conversion of sinners, for those who pierce my heart and the heart of my Son Jesus with the sword of hatred and daily blasphemies. Let us pray, little children, for all those who do not desire to come to know the love of God, even though they are in the Church. Let us pray that they convert, so that the Church may resurrect in love. Only with love and prayer, little children, can you live this time which is given to you for conversion. Place God in the first place, then the risen Jesus will become your friend. Thank you for having responded to my call."

April 25, 1999

"Dear children! Also today I call you to prayer. Little children, be joyful carriers of peace and love in this peaceless world. By fasting and prayer, witness that you are mine and that you live my messages. Pray and seek! I am praying and interceding for you before God that you convert; that your life and behavior always be Christian. Thank you for having responded to my call."

May 25, 1999

"Dear children! Also today I call you to convert and to more firmly believe in God. Children, you seek peace and pray in different ways, but you have not yet given your hearts to God for Him to fill them with His love. So, I am with you to teach you and to bring you closer to the love of God. If you love God above all else, it will be easy for you to pray and to open your hearts to Him. Thank you for having responded to my call."

June 25, 1999

"Dear children! Today I thank you for living and witnessing my messages with your life. Little children, be strong and pray so that prayer may give you strength and joy. Only in this way will each of you be mine and I will lead you on the way of salvation. Little children, pray and with your life witness my presence here. May each day be a joyful witness for you of God's love. Thank you for having responded to my call."

July 25, 1999

"Dear children! Also today I rejoice with you and I call you all to prayer with the heart. I call

all of you, little children, to give thanks to God here with me for the graces which He gives to you through me. I desire for you to comprehend that I want to realise here, not only a place of prayer but also a meeting of hearts. I desire for my, Jesus' and your heart to become one heart of love and peace. That is why, little children, pray and rejoice over everything that God does here, despite that Satan provokes quarrels and unrest. I am with you and I lead you all on the way of love. Thank you for having responded to my call."

August 25, 1999

"Dear children! Also today I call you to give glory to God the Creator in the colours of nature. He speaks to you also through the smallest flower about His beauty and the depth of love with which He has created you. Little children, may prayer flow from your hearts like fresh water from a spring. May the wheat fields speak to you about the mercy of God towards every creature. That is why, renew prayer of thanksgiving for everything He gives you. Thank you for having responded to my call."

September 25, 1999

"Dear children! Today again I call you to become carriers of my peace. In a special way, now when it is being said that God is far away, He has truly never been nearer to you. I call you to renew prayer in your families by reading the Sacred Scripture and to experience joy in meeting with God who infinitely loves His creatures. Thank you for having responded to my call."

October 25, 1999

"Dear children! Do not forget: this is a time of grace; that is why, pray, pray, pray! Thank you for having responded to my call."

November 25, 1999

"Dear children! Also today I call you to prayer. In this time of grace, may the cross be a sign-post of love and unity for you through which true peace comes. That is why, little children, pray especially at this time that little Jesus, the Creator of peace, may be born in your hearts. Only through prayer will you become my apostles of peace in this world without peace. That is why, pray until prayer becomes a joy for you. Thank you for having responded to my call."

December 25, 1999

"Dear children! This is the time of grace. Little children, today in a special way with little Jesus, whom I hold in my embrace, I am giving you the possibility to decide for peace. Through your 'yes' for peace and your decision for God, a new possibility for peace is opened. Only in this way, little children, this century will be for you a time of peace and well-being. Therefore, put little newborn Jesus in the first place in your life and He will lead you on the way of salvation. Thank you for having responded to my call."

2000

January 25, 2000

"Dear children! I call you, little children, to pray without ceasing. If you pray, you are closer to God and He will lead you on the way of peace and salvation. That is why I call you today to give peace to others. Only in God is there true peace. Open your hearts and become those who give a gift of peace and others will discover peace in you and through you and in this way you will witness God's peace and love which He gives you. Thank you for having responded to my call."

February 25, 2000

"Dear children! Wake up from the sleep of unbelief and sin, because this is a time of grace which God gives you. Use this time and seek the grace of healing of your heart from God, so that you may see God and man with the heart. Pray in a special way for those who have not come to know God's love, and witness with your life so that they also can come to know God and His immeasurable love. Thank you for having responded to my call."

March 25, 2000

"Dear children! Pray and make good use of this time, because this is a time of grace. I am with you and I intercede for each one of you before God, for your heart to open to God and to God's love. Little children, pray without ceasing, until prayer becomes a joy for you. Thank you for having responded to my call."

April 25, 2000

"Dear children! Also today I call you to conversion. You are concerned too much about material things and little about spiritual ones. Open your hearts and start again to work more on your personal conversion. Decide everyday to dedicate time to God and to prayer until prayer becomes a joyful meeting with God for you. Only in this way will your life have meaning and with joy you will contemplate eternal life. Thank you for having responded to my call."

May 25, 2000

"Dear children! I rejoice with you and in this time of grace I call you to spiritual renewal. Pray, little children, that the Holy Spirit may come to dwell in you in fullness, so that you may be able to witness in joy to all those who are far from faith. Especially, little children, pray for the gifts of the Holy Spirit so that in the spirit of love, every day and in each situation, you may be closer to your fellow-man; and that in wisdom and love you may overcome every difficulty. I am with you and I intercede for each of you before Jesus. Thank you for having responded to my call."

June 25, 2000

"Dear children! Today I call you to prayer. The one who prays is not afraid of the future. Little children do not forget, I am with you and I love you all. Thank you for having responded to my call."

July 25, 2000

"Dear children! Do not forget that you are here on earth on the way to eternity and that your home is in Heaven. That is why, little children, be open to God's love and leave egoism and sin. May your joy be only in discovering God in daily prayer. That is why, make good use of this time and pray, pray, pray; and God is near to you in prayer and through prayer. Thank you for having responded to my call."

August 25, 2000

"Dear children! I desire to share my joy with you. In my Immaculate Heart I feel that there are many of those who have drawn closer to me and are, in a special way, carrying the victory of my Immaculate Heart in their hearts by praying and converting. I desire to thank you and to inspire you to work even more for God and His kingdom with love and the power of the Holy Spirit. I am with you and I bless you with my motherly blessing. Thank you for having responded to my call."

September 25, 2000

"Dear children! Today I call you to open yourselves to prayer. May prayer become joy for you. Renew prayer in your families and form prayer groups. In this way, you will experience joy in prayer and togetherness. All those who pray and are members of prayer groups are open to God's will in their hearts and joyfully witness God's love. I am with you, I carry all of you in my heart and I bless you with my motherly blessing. Thank you for having responded to my call."

October 25, 2000

"Dear children! Today I desire to open my motherly heart to you and to call you all to pray for my intentions. I desire to renew prayer with you and to call you to fast which I desire to offer to my Son Jesus for the coming of a new time – a time of spring. In this Jubilee year many hearts have opened to me and the Church is being renewed in the Spirit. I rejoice with you and I thank God for this gift; and you, little children, I call to pray, pray, pray – until prayer becomes a joy for you. Thank you for having responded to my call."

November 25, 2000

"Dear children! Today when Heaven is near to you in a special way, I call you to prayer so that through prayer you place God in the first place. Little children, today I am near you and I bless each of you with my motherly blessing so that you have the strength and love for all the people you meet in your earthly life and that you can give God's love. I rejoice with you and I desire to tell you that your brother Slavko has been born into Heaven and intercedes for you. Thank you for having responded to my call."

December 25, 2000

"Dear children! Today when God granted to me that I can be with you, with little Jesus in my arms, I rejoice with you and I give thanks to God for everything He has done in this Jubilee year. I thank God especially for all the vocations of those who said 'yes' to God completely. I bless you all with my blessing and the blessing of the newborn Jesus. I pray for all of you for joy to be born in your hearts so that in joy you too carry the joy

I have today. In this Child I bring to you the Saviour of the your hearts and the One who calls you to the holiness of life. Thank you for having responded to my call."

2001

January 25, 2001

"Dear children! Today I call you to renew prayer and fasting with even greater enthusiasm until prayer becomes a joy for you. Little children, the one who prays is not afraid of the future and the one who fasts is not afraid of evil. Once again, I repeat to you: only through prayer and fasting also wars can be stopped – wars of your unbelief and fear for the future. I am with you and am teaching you little children: your peace and hope are in God. That is why draw closer to God and put Him in the first place in your life. Thank you for having responded to my call."

February 25, 2001

"Dear children! This is a time of grace. That is why pray, pray, pray until you comprehend God's love for each of you. Thank you for having responded to my call."

March 25, 2001

"Dear children! Also today I call you to open yourselves to prayer. Little children, you live in a time in which God gives great graces but you do not know how to make good use of them. You are concerned about everything else, but the least for the soul and spiritual life. Awaken from the tired sleep of your soul and say yes to God with all your strength. Decide for conversion and holiness. I am with you, little children, and I call you to perfection of your soul and of everything you do. Thank you for having responded to my call."

April 25, 2001

"Dear children! Also today, I call you to prayer. Little children, prayer works miracles. When you are tired and sick and you do not know the meaning of your life, take the Rosary and pray; pray until prayer becomes for you a joyful meeting with your Saviour. I am with you, little children, and I intercede and pray for you. Thank you for having responded to my call."

May 25, 2001

"Dear children! At this time of grace, I call you to prayer. Little children, you work much but without God's blessing. Bless and seek the wisdom of the Holy Spirit to lead you at this time so that you may comprehend and live in the grace of this time. Convert, little children, and kneel in the silence of your hearts. Put God in the center of your being so that, in that way, you can witness in joy the beauty that God continually gives in your life. Thank you for having responded to my call."

June 25, 2001

"Dear children! I am with you and I bless you all with my motherly blessing. Especially today when God gives you abundant graces, pray and seek God through me. God gives you great graces, that is why, little children make good use of this time of grace and come closer to my heart so that I can lead you to my Son Jesus. Thank you for having responded to my call."

July 25, 2001

"Dear children! In this time of grace, I call you to come even closer to God through your personal prayer. Make good use of the time of rest and give your soul and your eyes rest in God. Find peace in nature and you will discover God the Creator Whom you will be able to give thanks to for all creatures; then you will find joy in your heart. Thank you for having responded to my call."

August 25, 2001

"Dear children! Today I call all of you to decide for holiness. May for you, little children, always in your thoughts and in each situation holiness be in the first place, in work and in speech. In this way, you will also put it into practice; little by little, step by step, prayer and a decision for holiness will enter into your family. Be real with yourselves and do not bind yourselves to material things but to God. And do not forget, little chlidren, that your life is as passing as a flower. Thank you for having responded to my call."

September 25, 2001

"Dear children! Also today I call you to prayer, especially today when Satan wants war and hatred. I call you anew, little children: pray and fast that God may give you peace. Witness peace to every heart and be carriers of peace in this world without peace. I am with you and intercede before God for each of you. And you do not be afraid because the one who prays is not afraid of evil and has no hatred in the heart. Thank you for having responded to my call."

October 25, 2001

"Dear children! Also today I call you to pray from your whole heart and to love each other. Little children, you are chosen to witness peace and joy. If there is no peace, pray and you will receive it. Through you and your prayer, little children, peace will begin to flow through the world. That is why, little children, pray, pray, pray, because prayer works miracles in human hearts and in the world. I am with you and I thank God for each of you who has accepted and lives prayer with seriousness. Thank you for having responded to my call."

November 25, 2001

"Dear children! In this time of grace, I call you anew to prayer. Little children, pray and prepare your hearts for the coming of the King of Peace, that with His blessing He may give peace to the whole world. Peacelessness has begun to reign in hearts and hatred reigns in the world. That is why, you who live my messages be the light and extended hands to this faithless world that all may come to know the God of Love. Do not forget, little children, I am with you and bless you all. Thank you for having responded to my call."

December 25, 2001

"Dear children! I call you today and encourage you to prayer for peace. Especially today I call you, carrying the newborn Jesus in my arms for you, to unite with Him through prayer and to become a sign to this peaceless world. Encourage each other, little children, to prayer and love. May your faith be an encouragement to others to believe and to love more. I bless you all and call you to be closer to my heart and to the heart of little Jesus. Thank you for having responded to my call."

2002

January 25, 2002

"Dear children! At this time while you are still looking back to the past year I call you, little children, to look deeply into your heart and to decide to be closer to God and to prayer. Little children, you are still attached to earthly things and little to spiritual life. May my call today also be an encouragement to you to decide for God and for daily conversion. You cannot be converted, little children, if you do not abandon sins and do not decide for love towards God and neighbour. Thank you for having responded to my call."

February 25, 2002

"Dear children! In this time of grace, I call you to become friends of Jesus. Pray for peace in your hearts and work for your personal conversion. Little children, only in this way will you be able to become witnesses of peace and of the love of Jesus in the world. Open yourselves to prayer so that prayer becomes a need for you. Be converted, little children, and work so that as many souls as possible may come to know Jesus and His love. I am close to you and I bless you all. Thank you for having responded to my call."

March 25, 2002

"Dear children! Today I call you to unite with Jesus in prayer. Open your heart to Him and give Him everything that is in it: joys, sorrows and illnesses. May this be a time of grace for you. Pray, little children, and may every moment belong to Jesus. I am with you and I intercede for you. Thank you for having responded to my call."

April 25, 2002

"Dear children! Rejoice with me in this time of spring when all nature is awakening and your hearts long for change. Open yourselves, little children, and pray. Do not forget that I am with you and I desire to take you all to my Son that He may give you the gift of sincere love towards God and everything that is from Him. Open yourselves to prayer and seek a conversion of your hearts from God; everything else He sees and provides. Thank you for having responded to my call."

May 25, 2002

"Dear children! Today I call you to put prayer in the first place in your life. Pray and may prayer, little children, be a joy for you. I am with you and intercede for all of you, and you, little children, be joyful carriers of my messages. May your life with me be joy. Thank you for having responded to my call."

June 25, 2002

"Dear children! Today I pray for you and with you that the Holy Spirit may help you and increase your faith, so that you may accept even more the messages that I am giving you here in this holy place. Little children, comprehend that this is a time of grace for each of you; and with me, little children, you are secure. I desire to lead you all on the way of holiness. Live my messages and put into life every word that I am giving you. May they be precious to you because they come from heaven. Thank you for having responded to my call."

July 25, 2002

"Dear children! Today I rejoice with your patron saint and call you to be open to God's will, so that in you and through you, faith may grow in the people you meet in your everyday life. Little children, pray until prayer becomes joy for you. Ask your holy protectors to help you grow in love towards God. Thank you for having responded to my call.

August 25, 2002

"Dear children! Also today I am with you in prayer so that God gives you an even stronger faith. Little children, your faith is small and you are not even aware how much, despite this, you are not ready to seek the gift of faith from God. That is why I am with you, little children, to help you comprehend my messages and put them into life. Pray, pray, pray and only in faith and through prayer your soul will find peace and the world will find joy to be with God. Thank you for having responded to my call."

September 25, 2002

"Dear children! Also in this peaceless time, I call you to prayer. Little children, pray for peace so that in the world every person would feel love towards peace. Only when the soul finds peace in God, it feels content and love will begin to flow in the world. And in a special way, little children, you are called to live and witness peace – peace in your hearts and families – and, through you, peace will also begin to flow in the world. Thank you for having responded to my call."

October 25, 2002

"Dear children! Also today I call you to prayer. Little children, believe that by simple prayer miracles can be worked. Through your prayer you open your heart to God and He works miracles in your life. By looking at the fruits, your heart fills with joy and gratitude to God for everything He does in your life and, through you, also to others. Pray and believe little children, God gives you graces and you do not see them. Pray and you will see them. May your day be filled with prayer and thanksgiving for everything that God gives you. Thank you for having responded to my call."

November 25, 2002

"Dear children! I call you also today to conversion. Open your heart to God, little children, through Holy Confession and prepare your soul so that little Jesus can be born anew in your heart. Permit Him to transform you and lead you on the way of peace and joy. Little children, decide for prayer. Especially now, in this time of grace, may your heart yearn for prayer. I am close to you and intercede before God for all of you. Thank you for having responded to my call."

December 25, 2002

"Dear children! This is a time of great graces, but also a time of great trials for all those who desire to follow the way of peace. Because of that, little children, again I call you to pray, pray, pray, not with words but with the heart. Live my messages and be converted. Be conscious of this gift that God has permitted me to be with you, especially today when in my arms I have little Jesus - the King of Peace. I desire to give you peace, and that you carry it in your hearts and give it to others until God's peace begins to rule the world. Thank you for having responded to my call."

2003

January 25, 2003

"Dear children! With this message I call you anew to pray for peace. Particularly now when peace is in crisis, you be those who pray and bear witness to peace. Little children, be peace in this peaceless world. Thank you for having responded to my call."

February 25, 2003

"Dear children! Also today I call you to pray and fast for peace. As I have already said and now repeat to you, little children, only with prayer and fasting can wars also be stopped. Peace is a precious gift from God. Seek, pray and you will receive it. Speak about peace and carry peace in your hearts. Nurture it like a flower which is in need of water, tenderness and light. Be those who carry peace to others. I am with you and intercede for all of you. Thank you for having responded to my call."

March 25, 2003

"Dear children! Also today I call you to pray for peace. Pray with the heart, little children, and do not lose hope because God loves His creatures. He desires to save you, one by one, through my coming here. I call you to the way of holiness. Pray, and in prayer you are open to God's will; in this way, in everything you do, you realise God's plan in you and through you. Thank you for having responded to my call."

April 25, 2003

"Dear children! I call you also today to open yourselves to prayer. In the foregone time of Lent you have realised how small you are and how small your faith is. Little children, decide also today for God, that in you and through you He may change the hearts of people, and also your hearts. Be joyful carriers of the risen Jesus in this peaceless world, which yearns for God and for everything that is from God. I am with you, little children, and I love you with a special love. Thank you for having responded to my call."

May 25, 2003

"Dear children! Also today I call you to prayer. Renew your personal prayer, and in a special way pray to the Holy Spirit to help you pray with the heart. I intercede for all of you, little children, and call all of you to conversion. If you convert, all those around you will also be renewed and prayer will be a joy for them. Thank you for having responded to my call."

June 25, 2003

"Dear children! Also today, I call you with great joy to live my messages. I am with you and I thank you for putting into life what I am saying to you. I call you to renew my messages even more, with new enthusiasm and joy. May prayer be your daily practice. Thank you for having responded to my call."

July 25, 2003

"Dear children! Also today I call you to prayer. Little children, pray until prayer becomes a joy for you. Only in this way each of you will discover peace in the heart and your soul will be content. You will feel the need to witness to others the love that you feel in your heart and life. I am with you and intercede before God for all of you. Thank you for having responded to my call."

August 25, 2003

"Dear children! Also today I call you to give thanks to God in your heart for all the graces which He gives you, also through the signs and colours that are in nature. God wants to draw you closer to Himself and moves you to give Him glory and thanks. Therefore, little children, I call you anew to pray, pray, pray and do not forget that I am with you. I intercede before God for each of you until your joy in Him is complete. Thank you for having responded to my call."

September 25, 2003

"Dear children! Also today I call you to come closer to my heart. Only in this way, will you comprehend the gift of my presence here among you. I desire, little children, to lead you to the heart of my Son Jesus; but you resist and do not desire to open your hearts to prayer. Again, little children, I call you not to be deaf but to comprehend my call, which is salvation for you. Thank you for having responded to my call."

October 25, 2003

"Dear children! I call you anew to consecrate yourselves to my heart and the heart of my Son Jesus. I desire, little children, to lead you all on the way of conversion and holiness. Only in this way, through you, we can lead all the more souls on the way of salvation. Do not delay, little children, but say with all your heart: "I want to help Jesus and Mary that all the more brothers and sisters may come to know the way of holiness." In this way, you will feel the contentment of being friends of Jesus. Thank you for having responded to my call."

November 25, 2003

"Dear children! I call you that this time be for you an even greater incentive to prayer. In this time, little children, pray that Jesus be born in all hearts, especially in those who do not know Him. Be love, joy and peace in this peaceless world. I am with you and intercede before God for each of you. Thank you for having responded to my call."

December 25, 2003

"Dear children! Also today, I bless you all with my Son Jesus in my arms and I carry Him, who is the King of Peace, to you, that He grant you His peace. I am with you and I love you all, little children. Thank you for having responded to my call."

2004

January 25, 2004

"Dear children! Also today I call you to pray. Pray, little children, in a special way for all those who have not come to know God's love. Pray that their hearts may open and draw closer to my heart and the Heart of my Son Jesus, so that we can transform them into people of peace and love. Thank you for having responded to my call."

February 25, 2004

"Dear children! Also today, as never up to now, I call you to open your hearts to my messages.

Little children, be those who draw souls to God and not those who distance them. I am with you and love you all with a special love. This is a time of penance and conversion. From the bottom of my heart, I call you to be mine with all your heart and then you will see that your God is great, because He will give you an abundance of blessings and peace. Thank you for having responded to my call."

March 25, 2004

"Dear children! Also today, I call you to open yourselves to prayer. Especially now, in this time of grace, open your hearts, little children, and express your love to the Crucified. Only in this way, will you discover peace, and prayer will begin to flow from your heart into the world. Be an example, little children, and an incentive for the good. I am close to you and I love you all. Thank you for having responded to my call."

April 25, 2004

"Dear children! Also today, I call you to live my messages even more strongly in humility and love so that the Holy Spirit may fill you with His grace and strength. Only in this way will you be witnesses of peace and forgiveness. Thank you for having responded to my call."

May 25, 2004

"Dear children! Also today, I urge you to consecrate yourselves to my Heart and to the Heart of my Son Jesus. Only in this way will you be mine more each day and you will inspire each other all the more to holiness. In this way joy will rule your hearts and you will be carriers of peace and love. Thank you for having responded to my call."

June 25, 2004

"Dear children! Also today, joy is in my heart. I desire to thank you for making my plan realizable. Each of you is important, therefore, little children, pray and rejoice with me for every heart that has converted and become an instrument of peace in the world. Prayer groups are powerful, and through them I can see, little children, that the Holy Spirit is at work in the world. Thank you for having responded to my call."

July 25, 2004

"Dear children! I call you anew: be open to my messages. I desire, little children, to draw you all closer to my Son Jesus; therefore, you pray and fast. Especially I call you to pray for my intentions, so that I can present you to my Son Jesus; for Him to transform and open your hearts to love. When you will have love in the heart, peace will rule in you. Thank you for having responded to my call."

August 25, 2004

"Dear children! I call you all to conversion of heart. Decide, as in the first days of my coming here, for a complete change of your life. In this way, little children, you will have the strength to kneel and to open your hearts before God. God will hear your prayers and answer them. Before God, I intercede for each of you. Thank you for having responded to my call."

September 25, 2004

"Dear children! Also today, I call you to be love where there is hatred and food where there is hunger. Open your hearts, little children, and let your hands be extended and generous so that, through you, every creature may thank God the Creator. Pray, little children, and open your heart to God's love, but you cannot if you do not pray. Therefore, pray, pray, pray. Thank you for having responded to my call."

October 25, 2004

"Dear children! This is a time of grace for the family and, therefore, I call you to renew prayer. May Jesus be in the heart of your family. In prayer, learn to love everything that is holy. Imitate the lives of saints so that they may be an incentive and teachers on the way of holiness. May every family become a witness of love in this world without prayer and peace. Thank you for having responded to my call."

November 25, 2004

"Dear children! At this time, I call you all to pray for my intentions. Especially, little children, pray for those who have not yet come to know the love of God and do not seek God the Saviour. You, little children, be my extended hands and by your example draw them closer to my Heart and the Heart of my Son. God will reward you with graces and every blessing. Thank you for having responded to my call."

December 25, 2004

"Dear children! With great joy, also today I carry my Son Jesus in my arms to you; He blesses you and calls you to peace. Pray, little children, and be courageous witnesses of Good News in every situation. Only in this way will God bless you and give you everything you ask of Him in faith. I am with you as long as the Almighty permits me. I intercede for each of you with great love. Thank you for having responded to my call."

2005

January 25, 2005

"Dear children! In this time of grace again I call you to prayer. Pray, little children, for unity of Christians, that all may be one heart. Unity will really be among you in-as-much as you will pray and forgive. Do not forget: love will conquer only if you pray, and your heart will open. Thank you for having responded to my call."

February 25, 2005

"Dear children! Today I call you to be my extended hands in this world that puts God in the last place. You, little children, put God in the first place in your life. God will bless you and give you strength to bear witness to Him, the God of love and peace. I am with you and intercede for all of you. Little children, do not forget that I love you with a tender love. Thank you for having responded to my call."

March 25, 2005

"Dear children! Today I call you to love. Little children, love each other with God's love. At every moment, in joy and in sorrow, may love prevail and, in this way, love will begin to reign in your hearts. The risen Jesus will be with you and you will be His witnesses. I will rejoice with you and protect you with my motherly mantle. Especially, little children, I will watch your daily conversion with love. Thank you for having responded to my call."

April 25, 2005

"Dear children! Also today, I call you to renew prayer in your families. By prayer and the reading of Sacred Scripture, may the Holy Spirit, who will renew you, enter into your families. In this way, you will become teachers of the faith in your family. By prayer and your love, the world will set out on a better way and love will begin to rule in the world. Thank you for having responded to my call."

May 25, 2005

"Dear children! Anew I call you to live my messages in humility. Especially witness them now when we are approaching the anniversary of my apparitions. Little children, be a sign to those who are far from God and His love. I am with you and bless you all with my motherly blessing. Thank you for having responded to my call."

June 25, 2005

"Dear children! Today I thank you for every sacrifice that you have offered for my intentions. I call you, little children, to be my apostles of peace and love in your families and in the world. Pray that the Holy Spirit may enlighten and lead you on the way of holiness. I am with you and bless you all with my motherly blessing. Thank you for having responded to my call."

July 25, 2005

"Dear children! Also today, I call you to fill your day with short and ardent prayers. When you pray, your heart is open and God loves you with a special love and gives you special graces. Therefore, make good use of this time of grace and devote it to God more than ever up to now. Do novenas of fasting and renunciation so that Satan be far from you and grace be around you. I am near you and intercede before God for each of you. Thank you for having responded to my call."

August 25, 2005

"Dear children! Also today I call you to live my messages. God gave you a gift of this time as a time of grace. Therefore, little children, make good use of every moment and pray, pray, pray. I bless you all and intercede before the Most High for each of you. Thank you for having responded to my call."

September 25, 2005

"Dear children! In love I call you: convert, even though you are far from my heart. Do not forget, I am your mother and I feel pain for each one who is far from my heart; but I do not leave you alone. I believe you can leave the way of sin and decide for holiness. Thank you for having responded to my call."

October 25, 2005

"Little children, believe, pray and love, and God will be near you. He will give you the gift of all the graces you seek from Him. I am a gift to you, because, from day to day, God permits me to be with you and to love each of you with immeasurable love. Therefore, little children, in prayer and humility, open your hearts and be witnesses of my presence. Thank you for having responded to my call."

November 25, 2005

"Dear children! Also today I call you to pray, pray, pray until prayer becomes life for you. Little children, at this time, in a special way, I pray before God to give you the gift of faith. Only in faith will you discover the joy of the gift of life that God has given you. Your heart will be joyful thinking of eternity. I am with you and love you with a tender love. Thank you for having responded to my call."

December 25, 2005

"Dear children! Also today, in my arms I bring you little Jesus, the King of Peace, to bless you with His peace. Little children, in a special way today I call you to be my carriers of peace in this peaceless world. God will bless you. Little children, do not forget that I am your mother. I bless you all with a special blessing, with little Jesus in my arms. Thank you for having responded to my call."

2006

January 25, 2006

"Dear children! Also today I call you to be carriers of the Gospel in your families. Do not forget, little children, to read Sacred Scripture. Put it in a visible place and witness with your life that you believe and live the Word of God. I am close to you with my love and intercede before my Son for each of you. Thank you for having responded to my call."

February 25, 2006

"Dear children! In this Lenten time of grace, I call you to open your hearts to the gifts that God desires to give you. Do not be closed, but with prayer and renunciation say 'yes' to God and He will give to you in abundance. As in springtime the earth opens to the seed and yields a hundredfold, so also your heavenly Father will give to you in abundance. I am with you and love you, little children, with a tender love. Thank you for having responded to my call."

March 25, 2006

"Courage, little children! I decided to lead you on the way of holiness. Renounce sin and set out on the way of salvation, the way which my Son has chosen. Through each of your tribulations and sufferings God will find the way of joy for you. Therefore, little children, pray. We are close to you with our love. Thank you for having responded to my call."

April 25, 2006

"Dear children! Also today I call you to have more trust in me and my Son. He has conquered by His death and resurrection and, through me, calls you to be a part of His joy. You do not see God, little children, but if you pray you will feel His nearness. I am with you and intercede before God for each of you. Thank you for having responded to my call."

May 25, 2006

"Dear children! Also today I call you to put into practice and to live my messages that I am giving you. Decide for holiness, little children, and think of heaven. Only in this way, will you have peace in your heart that no one will be able to destroy. Peace is a gift, which God gives you in prayer. Little children, seek and work with all your strength for peace to win in your hearts and in the world. Thank you for having responded to my call."

June 25, 2006

"Dear children! With great joy in my heart I thank you for all the prayers that, in these days, you offered for my intentions. Know, little children, that you will not regret it, neither you nor your children. God will reward you with great graces and you will merit eternal life. I am near you and thank all those who, through these years, have accepted my messages, have poured them into your life and decided for holiness and peace. Thank you for having responded to my call."

July 25, 2006

"Dear children! At this time, do not only think of rest for your body but, little children, seek time also for the soul. In silence may the Holy Spirit speak to you and permit Him to convert and change you. I am with you and before God I intercede for each of you. Thank you for having responded to my call."

August 25, 2006

"Dear children! Also today I call you to pray, pray, pray. Only in prayer will you be near to me and my Son and you will see how short this life is. In your heart a desire for Heaven will be born. Joy will begin to rule in your heart and prayer will begin to flow like a river. In your words there will only be thanksgiving to God for having created you and the desire for holiness will become a reality for you. Thank you for having responded to my call."

September 25, 2006

"Dear children! Also today I am with you and call all of you to complete conversion. Decide for God, little children, and you will find in God the peace your heart seeks. Imitate the lives of saints and may they be an example for you; and I will inspire you as long as the Almighty permits me to be with you. Thank you for having responded to my call."

October 25, 2006

"Dear children! Today the Lord permitted me to tell you again that you live in a time of grace. You are not conscious, little children, that God is giving you a great opportunity to convert and to live in peace and love. You are so blind and attached to earthly things and think of earthly life. God sent me to lead you to eternal life. I, little children, am not tired, although I see that your hearts are heavy and tired for everything that is a grace and a gift. Thank you for having responded to my call."

November 25, 2006

"Dear children. Also today I call you to pray, pray, pray. Little children, when you pray you are close to God and He gives you the desire for eternity. This is a time when you can speak more about God and do more for God. Therefore, little children, do not resist but permit Him to lead you, to change you, and to enter into your life. Do not forget that you are travellers on the way toward eternity. Therefore, little children, permit God to lead you as a shepherd leads his flock. Thank you for having responded to my call."

December 25, 2006

"Dear children! Also today I bring you the newborn Jesus in my arms. He who is the King of Heaven and earth, He is your peace. Little children no one can give you peace as He who is the King of Peace. Therefore, adore Him in your hearts, chose Him and you will have joy in Him. He will bless you with His blessing of peace. Thank you for having responded to my call."

2007

January 25, 2007

"Dear children! Put Sacred Scripture in a visible place in your family and read it. In this way, you will come to know prayer with the heart and your thoughts will be on God. Do not forget that you are passing like a flower in a field, which is visible from afar, but disappears in a moment. Little children, leave a sign of goodness and love wherever you pass and God will bless you with an abundance of His blessing. Thank you for having responded to my call."

February 25, 2007

"Dear children! Open your heart to God's mercy in this Lenten time. The Heavenly Father desires to deliver each of you from the slavery of sin. Therefore, little children, make good use of this time and through meeting God in Confession, leave sin and decide for holiness. Do this out of love for Jesus, who redeemed you all with His blood, that you may be happy and in peace. Do not forget, little children: your freedom is your weakness, therefore follow my messages with seriousness. Thank you for having responded to my call."

March 25, 2007

"Dear children! I desire to thank you from my heart for your Lenten renunciations. I desire to inspire you to continue to live fasting with an open heart. By fasting and renunciation, little children, you will be stronger in faith. In God you will find true peace through daily prayer. I am with you and I am not tired. I desire to take you all with me to Heaven, therefore decide daily for holiness. Thank you for having responded to my call."

April 25, 2007

"Dear children! Also today I again call you to conversion. Open your hearts. This is a time of grace while I am with you, make good use of it. Say: "This is the time for my soul". I am with you and love you with immeasurable love. Thank you for having responded to my call."

May 25, 2007

"Dear children! Pray with me to the Holy Spirit for Him to lead you in the search of God's will on the way of your holiness. And you, who are far from prayer, convert and, in the silence of your heart, seek salvation for your soul and nurture it with prayer. I bless you all individually with my motherly blessing. Thank you for having responded to my call."

June 25, 2007

"Dear children! Also today, with great joy in my heart, I call you to conversion. Little children, do not forget that you are all important in this great plan, which God leads through Medjugorje. God desires to convert the entire world and to call it to salvation and to the way towards Himself, Who is the beginning and the end of every being. In a special way, little children, from the depth of my heart, I call you all to open yourselves to this great grace that God gives you through my presence here. I desire to thank each of you for the sacrifices and prayers. I am with you and I bless you all. Thank you for having responded to my call."

July 25, 2007

"Dear children! Today, on the day of the Patron of your Parish, I call you to imitate the lives of the saints. May they be, for you, an example and encouragement to a life of holiness. May prayer for you be like the air you breathe in and not a burden. Little children, God will reveal His love to you and you will experience the joy that you are my beloved. God will bless you and give you an abundance of grace. Thank you for having responded to my call."

August 25, 2007

"Dear children! Also today I call you to conversion. May your life, little children, be a reflection of God's goodness and not of hatred and unfaithfulness. Pray, little children, that prayer may become life for you. In this way, in your life you will discover the peace and joy which God gives to those who have an open heart to His love. And you who are far from God's mercy, convert so that God may not become deaf to your prayers and that it may not be too late for you. Therefore, in this time of grace, convert and put God in the first place in your life. Thank you for having responded to my call."

September 25, 2007

"Dear children! Also today I call all of you for your hearts to blaze with more ardent love for the Crucified, and do not forget that, out of love for you, He gave His life so that you may be saved. Little children, meditate and pray that your hearts may open to God's love. Thank you for having responded to my call."

October 25, 2007

"Dear children! God sent me among you out of love that I may lead you towards the way of salvation. Many of you opened your hearts and accepted my messages, but many have become lost on this way and have never come to know the God of love with the fullness of heart. Therefore, I call you to be love and light where there is darkness and sin. I am with you and bless you all. Thank you for having responded to my call."

November 25, 2007

Dear children! Today, when you celebrate Christ, the King of all that is created, I desire for Him to be the King of your lives. Only through giving, little children, can you comprehend the gift of Jesus' sacrifice on the Cross for each of you. Little children, give time to God that He may transform you and fill you with His grace, so that you may be a grace for others. For you, little children, I am a gift of grace and love, which comes from God for this peaceless world. Thank you for having responded to my call."

December 25, 2007

Dear children! With joy I bring you the King of peace for Him to bless you with His blessing. Adore Him and give to the Creator for whom your heart yearns. Do not forget that you are passers-by on this earth and that things can give you small joys, while through my Son, eternal life is given to you. That is why I am with you, to lead you towards what your heart yearns for. Thank you for having responded to my call."

2008

January 25, 2008

"Dear children! With the time of Lent, you are approaching a time of grace. Your heart is like ploughed soil and it is ready to receive the fruit which will grow into what is good. You, little children, are free to choose good or evil. Therefore, I call you to pray and fast. Plant joy and the fruit of joy will grow in your hearts for your good, and others will see it and receive it through your life. Renounce sin and choose eternal life. I am with you and intercede for you before my Son. Thank you for having responded to my call."

February 25, 2008

"Dear children! In this time of grace, I call you anew to prayer and renunciation. May your day be interwoven with little ardent prayers for all those who have not come to know God's love. Thank you for having responded to my call."

March 25, 2008

"Dear children! I call you to work on your personal conversion. You are still far from meeting with God in your heart. Therefore, spend all the more time in prayer and Adoration of Jesus in the Most Blessed Sacrament of the Altar, for Him to change you and to put into your hearts a living faith and a desire for eternal life. Everything is passing, little children, only God is not passing. I am with you and I encourage you with love. Thank you for having responded to my call."

April 25, 2008

"Dear children! Also today, I call all of you to grow in God's love as a flower which feels the warm rays of spring. In this way, also you, little children, grow in God's love and carry it to all those who are far from God. Seek God's will and do good to those whom God has put on your way, and be light and joy. Thank you for having responded to my call."

May 25, 2008

"Dear children! In this time of grace, when God has permitted me to be with you, little children, I call you anew to conversion. Work on the salvation of the world in a special way while I am with you. God is merciful and gives special graces, therefore, seek them through prayer. I am with you and do not leave you alone. Thank you for having responded to my call."

June 25, 2008

"Dear children! Also today, with great joy in my heart, I call you to follow me and to listen to my messages. Be joyful carriers of peace and love in this peaceless world. I am with you and I bless you all with my Son Jesus, the King of Peace. Thank you for having responded to my call."

July 25, 2008

"Dear children! At this time when you are thinking of physical rest, I call you to conversion. Pray and work so that your heart yearns for God the Creator who is the true rest of your soul and your body. May He reveal His face to you and may He give you His peace. I am with you and intercede before God for each of you. Thank you for having responded to my call."

August 25, 2008

"Dear children! Also today I call you to personal conversion. You be those who will convert and, with your life, will witness, love, forgive and bring the joy of the Risen One into this world, where my Son died and where people do not feel a need to seek Him and to discover Him in their lives. You adore Him, and may your hope be hope to those hearts who do not have Jesus. Thank you for having responded to my call."

September 25, 2008

"Dear children! May your life, anew, be a decision for peace. Be joyful carriers of peace and do not forget that you live in a time of grace, in which God gives you great graces through my presence. Do not close yourselves, little children, but make good use of this time and seek the gift of peace and love for your life so that you may become witnesses to others. I bless you with my motherly blessing. Thank you for having responded to my call."

October 25, 2008

"Dear children! In a special way I call you all to pray for my intentions so that, through your prayers, you may stop Satan's plan over this world, which is further from God every day, and which puts itself in the place of God and is destroying everything that is beautiful and good in the souls of each of you. Therefore, little children, arm yourselves with prayer and fasting so that you may be conscious of how much God loves you, and carry out God's will. Thank you for having responded to my call."

November 25, 2008

"Dear children! Also today I call you, in this time of grace, to pray for little Jesus to be born in your heart. May He, who is peace itself, give peace to the entire world through you. Therefore, little children, pray without ceasing for this turbulent world without hope, so that you may become witnesses of peace for all. May hope begin to flow through your hearts as a river of grace. Thank you for having responded to my call."

December 25, 2008

"Dear children! You are running, working, gathering – but without blessing. You are not praying! Today I call you to stop in front of the manger and to meditate on Jesus, Whom I give to you today also, to bless you and to help you to comprehend that, without Him, you have no future. Therefore, little children, surrender your lives into the hands of Jesus, for Him to lead you and protect you from every evil. Thank you for having responded to my call."

2009

January 25, 2009

"Dear children! Also today I call you to prayer. May prayer be for you like the seed that you will put in my heart, which I will give over to my Son Jesus for you, for the salvation of your souls. I desire, little children, for each of you to fall in love with eternal life which is your future, and for all worldly things to be a help for you to draw you closer to God the Creator. I am with you for this long because you are on the wrong path. Only with my help, little children, you will open your eyes. There are many of those who, by living my messages, comprehend that they are on the way of holiness towards eternity. Thank you for having responded to my call."

February 25, 2009

"Dear children! In this time of renunciation, prayer and penance, I call you anew: go and confess your sins so that grace may open your hearts, and permit it to change you. Convert little children, open yourselves to God and to His plan for each of you. Thank you for having responded to my call."

March 25, 2009

"Dear children! In this time of spring, when everything is awakening from the winter sleep, you also awaken your souls with prayer so that they may be ready to receive the light of the risen Jesus. Little children, may He draw you closer to His Heart so that you may become open to eternal life. I pray for you and intercede before the Most High for your sincere conversion. Thank you for having responded to my call."

April 25, 2009

"Dear children! Today I call you all to pray for peace and to witness it in your families so that peace may become the highest treasure on this peaceless earth. I am your Queen of Peace and your mother. I desire to lead you on the way of peace, which comes only from God. Therefore, pray, pray, pray. Thank you for having responded to my call."

May 25, 2009

"Dear children! In this time, I call you all to pray for the coming of the Holy Spirit upon every baptized creature, so that the Holy Spirit may renew you all and lead you on the way of witnessing your faith – you and all those who are far from God and His love. I am with you and intercede for you before the Most High. Thank you for having responded to my call."

June 25, 2009

"Dear children! Rejoice with me, convert in joy and give thanks to God for the gift of my presence among you. Pray that, in your hearts, God may be in the center of your life and with your life witness, little children, so that every creature may feel God's love. Be my extended hands for every creature, so that it may draw closer to the God of love. I bless you with my motherly blessing. Thank you for having responded to my call."

July 25, 2009

"Dear children! May this time be a time of prayer for you. Thank you for having responded to my call."

August 25, 2009

"Dear children! Today I call you anew to conversion. Little children, you are not holy enough and you do not radiate holiness to others, therefore pray, pray, pray and work on your personal conversion, so that you may be a sign of God's love to others. I am with you and am leading you towards eternity, for which every heart must yearn. Thank you for having responded to my call."

September 25, 2009

"Dear children, with joy, persistently work on your conversion. Offer all your joys and sorrows to my Immaculate Heart that I may lead you all to my most beloved Son, so that you may find joy in His Heart. I am with you to instruct you and to lead you towards eternity. Thank you for having responded to my call."

October 25, 2009

"Dear children! Also today I bring you my blessing, I bless you all and I call you to grow on this way, which God has begun through me for your salvation. Pray, fast and joyfully witness your faith, little children, and may your heart always be filled with prayer. Thank you for having responded to my call."

November 25, 2009

Dear children! In this time of grace I call you all to renew prayer in your families. Prepare yourselves with joy for the coming of Jesus. Little children, may your hearts be pure and pleasing, so that love and warmth may flow through you into every heart that is far from His love. Little children, be my extended hands, hands of love for all those who have become lost, who have no more faith and hope. Thank you for having responded to my call.

December 25, 2009

"Dear children! On this joyful day, I bring all of you before my Son, the King of Peace, that He may give you His peace and blessing. Little children, in love share that peace and blessing with others. Thank you for having responded to my call."

2010

January 25, 2010

"Dear children! May this time be a time of personal prayer for you, so that the seed of faith may grow in your hearts; and may it grow into a joyful witness to others. I am with you and I desire to inspire you all: grow and rejoice in the Lord Who has created you. Thank you for having responded to my call."

February 25, 2010

"Dear children! In this time of grace, when nature also prepares to give the most beautiful colors of the year, I call you, little children, to open your hearts to God the Creator for Him to transform and mould you in His image, so that all the good which has fallen asleep in your hearts may awaken to a new life and a longing towards eternity. Thank you for having responded to my call."

March 25, 2010

"Dear children! Also today I desire to call you all to be strong in prayer and in the moments when trials attack you. Live your Christian vocation in joy and humility and witness to everyone. I am with you and I carry you all before my Son Jesus, and He will be your strength and support. Thank you for having responded to my call."

April 25, 2010

"Dear children! At this time, when in a special way you are praying and seeking my intercession, I call you, little children, to pray so that through your prayers I can help you to have all the more hearts be opened to my messages. Pray for my intentions. I am with you and I intercede before my Son for each of you. Thank you for having responded to my call."

May 25, 2010

"Dear children! God gave you the grace to live and to defend all the good that is in you and around you, and to inspire others to be better and holier; but Satan, too, does not sleep and through modernism diverts you and leads you to his way. Therefore, little children, in the love for my Immaculate Heart, love God above everything and live His commandments. In this way, your life will have meaning and peace will rule on earth. Thank you for having responded to my call."

June 25, 2010

"Dear children! With joy, I call you all to live my messages with joy; only in this way, little children, will you be able to be closer to my Son. I desire to lead you all only to Him, and in Him you will find true peace and the joy of your heart. I bless you all and love you with immeasurable love. Thank you for having responded to my call."

July 25, 2010

"Dear children! Anew I call you to follow me with joy. I desire to lead all of you to my Son, your Savior. You are not aware that without Him you do not have joy and peace, nor a future or eternal life. Therefore, little children, make good use of this time of joyful prayer and surrender. Thank you for having responded to my call."

August 25, 2010

"Dear children! With great joy, also today, I desire to call you anew: pray, pray, pray. May this time be a time of personal prayer for you. During the day, find a place where you will pray joyfully in a recollected way. I love you and bless you all. Thank you for having responded to my call."

September 25, 2010

"Dear children! Today I am with you and bless you all with my motherly blessing of peace, and I urge you to live your life of faith even more, because you are still weak and are not humble. I urge you, little children, to speak less and to work more on your personal conversion so that your witness may be fruitful. And may your life be unceasing prayer. Thank you for having responded to my call."

October 25, 2010

"Dear children! May this time be a time of prayer for you. My call, little children, desires to be for you a call to decide to follow the way of conversion; therefore, pray and seek the intercession of all the saints. May they be for you an example, an incentive and a joy towards eternal life. Thank you for having responded to my call."

November 25, 2010

"Dear children! I look at you and I see in your heart death without hope, restlessness and hunger. There is no prayer or trust in God, that is why the Most High permits me to bring you hope and joy. Open yourselves. Open your hearts to God's mercy and He will give you everything you need and will fill your hearts with peace, because He is peace and your hope. Thank you for having responded to my call."

December 25, 2010

"Dear children! Today, I and my Son desire to give you an abundance of joy and peace so that each of you may be a joyful carrier and witness of peace and joy in the places where you live. Little children, be a blessing and be peace. Thank you for having responded to my call."

2011

January 25, 2011

"Dear children! Also today I am with you and I am looking at you and blessing you, and I am not losing hope that this world will change for the good and that peace will reign in the hearts of men. Joy will begin to reign in the world because you have opened yourselves to my call and to God's love. The Holy Spirit is changing a multitude of those who have said 'yes'. Therefore I desire to say to you: thank you for having responded to my call."

February 25, 2011

"Dear children! Nature is awakening and on the trees the first buds are seen which will bring most beautiful flowers and fruit. I desire that you also, little children, work on your conversion and that you be those who witness with their life, so that your example may be a sign and an incentive for conversion to others. I am with you and before my Son Jesus I intercede for your conversion. Thank you for having responded to my call."

March 25, 2011

"Dear children! In a special way today I desire to call you to conversion. As of today, may new life begin in your heart. Children, I desire to see your 'yes', and may your life be a joyful living of God's will at every moment of your life. In a special way today, I bless you with my motherly blessing of peace, love and unity in my heart and in the heart of my Son Jesus. Thank you for having responded to my call."

April 25, 2011

"Dear children! As nature gives the most beautiful colors of the year, I also call you to witness with your life and to help others to draw closer to my Immaculate Heart, so that the flame of love for the Most High may sprout in their hearts. I am with you and I unceasingly pray for you that your life may be a reflection of Heaven here on earth. Thank you for having responded to my call."

May 25, 2011

"Dear children! My prayer today is for all of you who seek the grace of conversion. You knock on the door of my heart, but without hope and prayer, in sin, and without the Sacrament of Reconciliation with God. Leave sin and decide, little children, for holiness. Only in this way can I help you, hear your prayers and seek intercession before the Most High. Thank you for having responded to my call."

June 25, 2011

"Dear children! Give thanks with me to the Most High for my presence with you. My heart is joyful watching the love and joy in the living of my messages. Many of you have responded, but I wait for, and seek, all the hearts that have fallen asleep to awaken from the sleep of unbelief. Little children, draw even closer to my Immaculate Heart so that I can lead all of you toward eternity. Thank you for having responded to my call."

July 25, 2011

"Dear children! May this time be for you a time of prayer and silence. Rest your body and spirit, may they be in God's love. Permit me, little children, to lead you, open your hearts to the Holy Spirit so that all the good that is in you may blossom and bear fruit one hundred fold. Begin and end the day with prayer with the heart. Thank you for having responded to my call."

August 25, 2011

"Dear children! Today I call you to pray and fast for my intentions, because satan wants to destroy my plan. Here I began with this parish and invited the entire world. Many have responded, but there is an enormous number of those who do not want to hear or accept my call. Therefore, you who have said 'yes', be strong and resolute. Thank you for having responded to my call."

September 25, 2011

"Dear children! I call you, for this time to be for all of you, a time of witnessing. You, who live in the love of God and have experienced His gifts, witness them with your words and life that they may be for the joy and encouragement to others in faith. I am with you and incessantly intercede before God for all of you that your faith may always be alive and joyful, and in the love of God. Thank you for having responded to my call."

October 25, 2011

"Dear children! I am looking at you and in your hearts I do not see joy. Today I desire to give you the joy of the Risen One, that He may lead you and embrace you with His love and tenderness. I love you and I am praying for your conversion without ceasing before my Son Jesus. Thank you for having responded to my call."

November 25, 2011

"Dear children! Today I desire to give you hope and joy. Everything that is around you, little children, leads you towards worldly things but I desire to lead you towards a time of grace, so that through this time you may be all the closer to my Son, that He can lead you towards His love and eternal life, for which every heart yearns. You, little children, pray and may this time for you be one of grace for your soul. Thank you for having responded to my call."

December 25, 2011

"Dear children! Also today, in my arms I am carrying my Son Jesus to you, for Him to give you His peace. Pray, little children, and witness so that in every heart, not human but God's peace may prevail, which no one can destroy. It is that peace in the heart which God gives to those whom He loves. By your baptism you are all, in a special way called and loved, therefore witness and pray that you may be my extended hands to this world which yearns for God and peace. Thank you for having responded to my call."

2012

January 25, 2012

"Dear children! With joy, also today I call you to open your hearts and to listen to my call. Anew, I desire to draw you closer to my Immaculate Heart, where you will find refuge and peace. Open yourselves to prayer, until it becomes a joy for you. Through prayer, the Most High will give you an abundance of grace and you will become my extended hands in this restless world which longs for peace. Little children, with your lives witness faith and pray that faith may grow day by day in your hearts. I am with you. Thank you for having responded to my call."

February 25, 2012

"Dear children! At this time, in a special way I call you: 'pray with the heart'. Little children, you speak much and pray little. Read and meditate on Sacred Scripture, and may the words written in it be life for you. I encourage and love you, so that in God you may find your peace and the joy of living. Thank you for having responded to my call."

March 25, 2012

"Dear children! Also today, with joy, I desire to give you my motherly blessing and to call you to prayer. May prayer become a need for you to grow more in holiness every day. Work more on your conversion because you are far away, little children. Thank you for having responded to my call."

25 April, 2012

"Dear children! Also today I am calling you to prayer, and may your heart, little children, open towards God as a flower opens towards the warmth of the sun. I am with you and I intercede for all of you. Thank you for having responded to my call."

25 May, 2012

"Dear children! Also today I call you to conversion and to holiness. God desires to give you joy and peace through prayer but you, little children, are still far away - attached to the earth and to earthly things. Therefore, I call you anew: open your heart and your sight towards God and the things of God - and joy and peace will come to reign in your hearts. Thank you for having responded to my call."

25 June, 2012

"Dear children! With great hope in the heart, also today I call you to prayer. If you pray, little children, you are with me and you are seeking the will of my Son and are living it. Be open and live prayer and, at every moment, may it be for you the savor and joy of your soul. I am with you and I intercede for all of you before my Son Jesus. Thank you for having responded to my call."

25 July, 2012

"Dear children! Today I call you to the 'good'. Be carriers of peace and goodness in this world. Pray that God may give you the strength so that hope and pride may always reign in your heart and life because you are God's children and carriers of His hope to this world that is without joy in the heart, and is without a future, because it does not have its heart open to God who is your salvation. Thank you for having responded to my call."

25 August, 2012

"Dear children! Also today, with hope in the heart, I am praying for you and am thanking the Most High for every one of you who lives my messages with the heart. Give thanks to God's love that I can love and lead each of you through my Immaculate Heart also toward conversion. Open your hearts and decide for holiness, and hope will give birth to joy in your hearts. Thank you for having responded to my call."

25 September, 2012

"Dear children! When in nature you look at the richness of the colors which the Most High gives to you, open your heart and pray with gratitude for all the good that you have and say: 'I am here created for eternity' – and yearn for heavenly things because God loves you with immeasurable love. This is why He also gave me to you to tell you: 'Only in God is your peace and hope, dear children'. Thank you for having responded to my call."

25 October, 2012

"Dear children! Today I call you to pray for my intentions. Renew fasting and prayer because Satan is cunning and attracts many hearts to sin and perdition. I call you, little children, to holiness and to live in grace. Adore my Son so that He may fill you with His peace and love for which you yearn. Thank you for having responded to my call."

25 November, 2012

"Dear children! In this time of grace, I call all of you to renew prayer. Open yourselves to Holy Confession so that each of you may accept my call with the whole heart. I am with you and I protect you from the ruin of sin, but you must open yourselves to the way of conversion and holiness, that your heart may burn out of love for God. Give Him time and He will give Himself to you and thus, in the will of God you will discover the love and the joy of living. Thank you for having responded to my call."

25 December, 2012

Our Lady came with little Jesus in her arms and she did not give a message, but little Jesus began to speak and said: "I am your peace, live my commandments." With a sign of the cross, Our Lady and little Jesus blessed us together.

2013

25 January, 2013

"Dear children! Also today I call you to prayer. May your prayer be as strong as a living stone, until with your lives you become witnesses. Witness the beauty of your faith. I am with you and intercede before my Son for each of you. Thank you for having responded to my call."

25 February, 2013

"Dear children! Also today I call you to prayer. Sin is pulling you towards worldly things and I have come to lead you towards holiness and the things of God, but you are struggling and spending your energies in the battle with the good and the evil that are in you. Therefore, little children, pray, pray, pray until prayer becomes a joy for you and your life will become a simple walk towards God. Thank you for having responded to my call."

25 March, 2013

"Dear children! In this time of grace I call you to take the cross of my beloved Son Jesus in your hands and to meditate on His passion and death. May your suffering be united in His suffering and love will win, because He who is love gave Himself out of love to save each of you. Pray, pray, pray until love and peace begin to reign in your hearts. Thank you for having responded to my call."

April 25, 2013

"Dear children! Pray, pray, keep praying until your heart opens in faith as a flower opens to the warm rays of the sun. This is a time of grace which God gives you through my presence but you are far from my heart, therefore, I call you to personal conversion and to family prayer. May Sacred Scripture always be an incentive for you. I bless you all with my motherly blessing. Thank you for having responded to my call."

May 25, 2013

"Dear children! Today I call you to be strong and resolute in faith and prayer, until your prayers are so strong so as to open the Heart of my beloved Son Jesus. Pray little children, pray without ceasing until your heart opens to God's love. I am with you and I intercede for all of you and I pray for your conversion. Thank you for having responded to my call."

June 25, 2013

"Dear children! With joy in the heart I love you all and call you to draw closer to my Immaculate Heart so I can draw you still closer to my Son Jesus, and that He can give you His peace and love, which are nourishment for each one of you. Open yourselves, little children, to prayer – open yourselves to my love. I am your mother and cannot leave you alone in wandering and sin. You are called, little children, to be my children, my beloved children, so I can present you all to my Son. Thank you for having responded to my call."

July 25, 2013

"Dear children! With joy in my heart I call all of you to live your faith and to witness it with your heart and by your example in every way. Decide, little children, to be far from sin and temptation and may there be joy and love for holiness in your hearts. I love you, little children, and accompany you with my intercession before the Most High. Thank you for having responded to my call."

August 25, 2013

"Dear children! Also today, the Most High is giving me the grace to be with you and to lead you towards conversion. Every day I am sowing and am calling you to conversion, that you may be prayer, peace, love - the grain that by dying will give birth a hundredfold. I do not desire for you, dear children, to have to repent for everything that you could have done but did not want to. Therefore, little children, again, with enthusiasm say: 'I want to be a sign to others.' Thank you for having responded to my call."

September 25, 2013

"Dear children! Also today I call you to prayer. May your relationship with prayer be a daily one. Prayer works miracles in you and through you, therefore, little children, may prayer be a joy for you. Then your relationship with life will be deeper and more open and you will comprehend that life is a gift for each of you. Thank you for having responded to my call."

October 25, 2013

"Dear children! Today I call you to open yourselves to prayer. Prayer works miracles in you and through you. Therefore, little children, in the simplicity of heart seek of the Most High to give you the strength to be God's children and for Satan not to shake you like the wind shakes the branches. Little children, decide for God anew and seek only His will – and then you will find joy and peace in Him. Thank you for having responded to my call."

25 November 25, 2013

"Dear children! Today I call all of you to prayer. Open the doors of your heart profoundly to prayer, little children, to prayer with the heart; and then the Most High will be able to act upon your freedom and conversion will begin. Your faith will become firm so that you will be able to say with all your heart: 'My God, my all.' You will comprehend, little children, that here on earth everything is passing. Thank you for having responded to my call."

December 25, 2013

"Dear children! I am carrying to you the King of Peace that He may give you His peace. You, little children, pray, pray, pray. The fruit of prayer will be seen on the faces of the people who have decided for God and His Kingdom. I, with my Son Jesus, bless you all with a blessing of peace. Thank you for having responded to my call."

2014

January 25, 2014

"Dear children! Pray, pray, pray for the radiance of your prayer to have an influence on those whom you meet. Put the Sacred Scripture in a visible place in your families and read it, so that the words of peace may begin to flow in your hearts. I am praying with you and for you, little children, that from day to day you may become still more open to God's will. Thank you for having responded to my call."

February 25, 2014

"Dear children! You see, hear and feel that in the hearts of many people there is no God. They do not want Him, because they are far from prayer and do not have peace. You, little children, pray - live God's commandments. You be prayer, you who from the very beginning said `yes` to my call. Witness God and my presence and do not forget, little children: I am with you and I love you. From day to day I present you all to my Son Jesus. Thank you for having responded to my call."

March 25, 2014

"Dear children! I am calling you anew: begin the battle against sin as in the first days, go to confession and decide for holiness. The love of God will begin to flow through you into the world, peace will begin to rule in your hearts and God's blessing will fill you. I am with you and intercede for all of you before my Son Jesus. Thank you for having responded to my call."

April 25, 2014

"Dear children! Open your hearts to the grace which God is giving you through me, as a flower that opens to the warm rays of the sun. Be prayer and love for all those who are far from God and His love. I am with you and I intercede for all of you before my Son Jesus, and I love you with immeasurable love. Thank you for having responded to my call."

May 25, 2014

"Dear children! Pray and be aware that without God you are dust. Therefore, turn your thoughts and heart to God and to prayer. Trust in His love. In God's spirit, little children, you are all called to be witnesses. You are precious and I call you, little children, to holiness, to eternal life. Therefore, be aware that this life is passing. I love you and call you to a new life of conversion. Thank you for having responded to my call."

June 25, 2014

"Dear children! The Most High is giving me the grace that I can still be with you and to lead you in prayer towards the way of peace. Your heart and soul thirst for peace and love, for God and His joy. Therefore, little children, pray, pray, pray and in prayer you will discover the wisdom of living. I bless you all and intercede for each of you before my Son Jesus. Thank you for having responded to my call."

July 25, 2014

"Dear children! You are not aware of the graces that you are living at this time in which the Most High is giving you signs for you to open and convert. Return to God and to prayer, and may prayer begin to reign in your hearts, families and communities, so that the Holy Spirit may lead and inspire you to every day be more open to God's will and to His plan for each of you. I am with you and with the saints and angels intercede for you. Thank you for having responded to my call."

August 25, 2014

"Dear children! Pray for my intentions, because Satan wants to destroy my plan which I have here and to steal your peace. Therefore, little children, pray, pray, pray that God can act through each of you. May your hearts be open to God's will. I love you and bless you with my motherly blessing. Thank you for having responded to my call."

September 25, 2014

"Dear children! Also today I call you to also be like the stars, which by their light give light and beauty to others so they may rejoice. Little children, also you be the radiance, beauty, joy and peace – and especially prayer – for all those who are far from my love and the love of my Son Jesus. Little children, witness your faith and prayer in joy, in the joy of faith that is in your hearts; and pray for peace, which is a precious gift from God. Thank you for having responded to my call."

October 25, 2014

"Dear children! Pray in this time of grace and seek the intercession of all the saints who are already in the light. From day to day may they be an example and encouragement to you on the way of your conversion. Little children, be aware that your life is short and passing. Therefore, yearn for eternity and keep preparing your hearts in prayer. I am with you and intercede before my Son for each of you, especially for those who have consecrated themselves to me and to my Son. Thank you for having responded to my call. "

November 25, 2014

"Dear Children! In a special way, today I am calling you to prayer. Pray, little children, so that you may comprehend who you are and where you need to go. Be carriers of the good news and be people of good hope. Be love for all those who are without love. Little children, you will be everything and will achieve everything only if you pray and are open to God's will – to God who desires to lead you to eternal life. I am with you and intercede for you from day to day before my Son Jesus. Thank you for having responded to my call."

Diagram and Messages
Illustrating the Five Themes

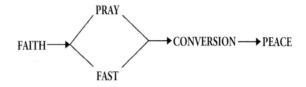

FAITH

"… I call you to renew in your families the fervour of the first days when I called you to fasting, prayer and conversion. …"

25 October 1998 (page 126)

"… I pray before God to give you the gift of faith. Only in faith will you discover the joy of the gift of life that God has given you. …"

25-11-2006 (page 155)

"… believe and pray that the Father increase your faith, and then ask for whatever you need…"

25-4-1988 (page 75)

"… There is no peace, little children, where there is no prayer and there is no love, where there is no faith. …"

25-3-1995 (page 109)

"… When you are far from God, you cannot receive graces because you do not seek them with a firm faith. …"

25-1-1988 (page 73)

"… I invite you to take the Cross in the hands and to meditate on the wounds of Jesus. Ask of Jesus to heal your wounds, which you, dear children, during your life sustained because of your sins or the sins of your parents. Only in this way, dear children, you will understand that the world is in need of healing of faith in God the Creator. …"

25-3-1997 (page 119)

"… your faith is small and you are not even aware how much, despite this, you are not ready to seek the gift of faith from God. … only in faith and through prayer your soul will find peace …"

25-8-2002 (page 143)

"… By Jesus' Passion and Death on the Cross, you will understand that only through prayer you, too, can become true apostles of faith; …"

25-3-1997 (page 119)

"… May your faith be an encouragement to others to believe and to love more. …"

25-12-2001 (page 140)

"… Open your hearts and surrender your life to Jesus so that He works through your hearts and strengthens you in faith. …"

23-5-1985 (page 41)

"… I wish that you all be the reflection of Jesus, which will enlighten this unfaithful world walking in darkness. …"

5-6-1986 (page 56)

"… begin to pray the Rosary with a living faith. That way I will be able to help you. …"

12-6-1986 (page 56)

"… Through prayer and your renunciation you will become more open to the gift of faith and love towards the Church and the people who are around you. …"

25-2-1998 (page 124)

PRAY

"… May prayer for you be like the air you breathe in and not a burden. …"

25-7-2007 (page 162)

"… prayer works miracles in human hearts and in the world. …" 25-10-2001 (page 139)

"… You wonder why all these prayers? Look around you, dear children, and you will see how greatly sin has dominated the world. Pray, therefore, that Jesus conquers. …"

13-9-1984 (page 30)

"… Pray, and then you shall overcome even every weariness. Prayer will be your joy and your rest. …" 30-5-85 (page41)

"… When trials and problems arise, you say, "O God! O Mother! Where are you?"

That is why, once more, please accept my call and start to pray in a new way until prayer becomes joy to you. …"

25-5-1992 (page 95)

"… When you pray you are much more beautiful, like flowers, which after the snow, show all their beauty and all their colours become indescribable. …"

18-12-1986 (page 65)

"… decide to consecrate time in the day only for an encounter with God in silence. …"

27-7-1989 (page 81)

"… I am with you and I wish to teach you to pray with the heart. In prayer with the heart you shall encounter God. …"

25-10-1989 (page 82)

"… find a corner for personal prayer. I desire to lead you towards prayer with the heart. Only in this way will you comprehend that your life is empty without prayer. …"

25-7-1997 (page 120)

"… fill your day with short and ardent prayers. …" 25-7-2005 (page 154)

"… if you do not pray, you cannot say that you are on the way to being converted. …"

25-6-92 (page 96)

"… The elderly are especially important in the family. Urge them to pray. …"

24-4-1986 (page 54)

"… Turn your hearts toward prayer and seek the Holy Spirit to be poured out on you. …"

9-5-1985 (page 40)

"… open to prayer so that in prayer the Holy Spirit will help you, that your hearts become of flesh and not of stone. …"

25-6-1996 (page 115)

"… pray daily for souls in purgatory. For every soul prayer and grace is necessary to reach God and the love of God. …"

6-11-1986 (page 63)

"… pray … that your Rosary be an obligation which you shall fulfill with joy. That way you shall understand the reason I am with you this long. I desire to teach you to pray. …"

12-6-1986 (page 56)

"… Pray all the prayers for the opening of sinful hearts. I desire that. God desires that through me. …"

18-4-1985 (page 39)

FAST

"… the one who prays is not afraid of the future and the one who fasts is not afraid of evil. …" 25-1-01 (page 136)

"…I desire to inspire you to continue to live fasting with an open heart. By fasting and renunciation,…you will be stronger in faith."

25-3-2007 (page 161)

"… Do novenas of fasting and renunciation so that Satan be far from you and grace be around you. …" 25-7-2005 (page 154)

"… Especially live the fasting, because with fasting you will give me the joy of seeing fulfilled all the plans which God has here in Medjugorje. …" 26-9-1985 (page 45)

"… pray without ceasing and prepare your hearts in penance and fasting. …"

4-12-1986 (page 65)

"… fast strictly on Wednesdays and Fridays, and every day to pray at least one Rosary: the joyful, sorrowful and glorious mysteries. …" Our Lady asked that we accept this message with a firm will. …" 14-8-1984 (page 29)

"… fast and pray with the heart. …"

20-9-1984 (page 30)

"… Only by prayer and fasting can war be stopped. …" 25-4-1992 (page 95)

"I would like the people to pray along with me these days. And to pray as much as possible! And to fast strictly on Wednesdays and Fridays, and every day to pray at least one Rosary; the joyful, sorrowful and glorious mysteries."

14-8-1984 (page ??)

Our Lady asked that we accept this message with a firm will. She especially requested this of the parishioners and the faithful of the surrounding places.

This message was given to Ivan in his home.

"….. Today I call on you to renew prayer and fasting with even greater enthusiasm until prayer becomes a joy for you. Little children, the one who prays is not afraid of the future and the one who fasts is not afraid of evil. Once again, I repeat to you: only through and fasting also wars can be stopped – wars of our unbelief and fear for the future. ...."

25-1-2001 (page ??)

CONVERSION

"... Today I invite you to conversion. This is the most important message I have given you here. ..." 25-2-1996 (page 113)

"... May Holy Confession be the first act of conversion for you and then decide for holiness." 25-11-1998 (page 127)

"... I am interceding for you before God that He gives you the gift of conversion of the heart. ..." 25-12-1989 (page 83)

"... make good use of this time and through meeting God in Confession, leave sin and decide for holiness. ..." 25-2-2007 (page 161)

"... I wish to call you all to confession, even if you have confessed a few days ago. ... I am inviting you all to reconciliation with God!"

24-3-1985 (page 38)

"... In silence may the Holy Spirit speak to you and permit Him to convert and change you. ..." 25-7-2006 (page 158)

"... seek with humility that which is not in order in your hearts, and you shall understand what you have to do. Conversion will become a daily duty that you will do with joy. ..."

25-4-1996 (page 114)

"... God can give you peace only if you convert and pray. ..."

25-5-1993 (page 101)

"... Conversion will be easy for all who desire to accept it. ..." 23-1-1986 (page 50)

"... I invite you to open the door of your heart to Jesus as a flower opens itself to the sun. Jesus desires to fill your hearts with peace and joy. ... Therefore, I invite you to Confession so Jesus may be your truth and peace. ..."

25-1-1995 (page 108)

"... This is a time of penance and conversion. From the bottom of my heart, I call you to be mine with all your heart and then you will see that your God is great, because He will give you an abundance of blessings and peace. ..."

25-2-2004 (page 149)

"... I wish to renew you and lead you with my Heart to the Heart of Jesus, which still today suffers for you and calls you to conversion and renewal. Through you I wish to renew the world. ... I invite you and I love you and in a special way implore: Convert! ..."

25-10-1996 (page 117)

PEACE

On the third day Our Lady appeared one more time to Marija only, coming down

Podbrdo, saying to her: "Peace, peace, peace and only peace." and repeated, in tears, "Peace must reign between man and God and between all people!"   26-6-1981 (page 11)

"… I am bringing peace to you I am your Mother, the Queen of Peace. …"

25-7-1988 (page 76)

"…You cannot have peace if your heart is not at peace with God. That is why, little children, pray, pray, pray, because prayer is the foundation of your peace. …"

25-6-1997 (page 120)

"… In God you will find true peace through daily prayer. I am with you and I am not tired." 23-3-2007 (page 161)

"… God is peace itself. Therefore, approach Him through your personal prayer and then live peace in your hearts and in this way peace will flow from your hearts like a river into the whole world. Do not speak about peace, but make peace. …" 25-2-91 (page 89)

"… God loves you with such a great love because He permits me to be with you so I can instruct you and help you to find the way of peace. This way, however, you cannot discover if you do not pray. …" 25-3-1988 (page 74)

"… you are chosen to witness peace and joy. If there is no peace, pray and you will receive it. …" 25-10-2001 (page 139)

"… I desire that each of you reflect and carry

peace in your heart and say: I want to put God in the first place in my life. …"

25-12-1997 (page 123)

"I call you to pray for peace. Without your prayers, dear children, I cannot help you to fulfill the message which the Lord has given me to give to you. …" 23-10-1986 (page 62)

"… Today I thank you and I want to invite you all to God's peace. I want each one of you to experience in your heart that peace which God gives. …" 25-6-1970 (page 70)

"… put God in the first place in your families, so that He may give you peace and may protect you not only from war, but also in peace protect you from every satanic attack. When God is with you, you have everything.…"

25-12-1991 (page 93)

"… I call you to peace. Live it in your heart and all around you, so that all will know peace, peace that does not come from you but from God. …" 25-12-1988 (page 78)

"… I wish to fill you with peace, joy and love of God. …" 20-6-1985 (page 42)

"… God is allowing me along with Himself to bring about this oasis of peace. I wish to call on you to protect it and that the oasis always be unspoiled. …" 26-6-1986 (page 57)

"… Pray for peace in your hearts and work for your personal conversion. …"

25-2-2002 (page 141)

"… without love you cannot live peace. The fruit of peace is love and the fruit of love is forgiveness. …" 25-1-1996 (page 113)

"…You know that I love you and am coming here out of love so I could show you the path to peace and salvation for your souls. I want you to obey me and not permit Satan to seduce you. …" 25-2-1988 (page 73)

"Unceasingly adore the Most Blessed Sacrament of the Altar. I am always present when the faithful are adoring. Special graces are then being received." (15-3-1984)

The Importance of The Messages

"… I am near you and thank all those who, through these years, have accepted my messages, have poured them into your life and decided for holiness and peace. …"

25-6-2006 (page 158)

"…You are the ones responsible for the messages. The source of grace is here, but you, dear children, are the vessels which transport the gifts. …I am calling you to do your job with responsibility. Each one shall be responsible according to his own ability. …I am calling you to give the gifts to others with love, and not to keep them for yourselves. …"

8-5-1986 (Page 54)

"…You are not conscious of the messages which God is sending you through me. He is giving you great graces and you do not comprehend them. Pray to the Holy Spirit for enlightenment. …" 8-11-1984 (Page 32)

"… In God's Name many times I have been giving you messages, but you have not listened to me. …" 6-12-1984 (Page 33)

"… I call you with great joy to live my messages. I am with you and I thank you for putting into life what I am saying to you. I call you to renew my messages even more, with new enthusiasm and joy. …" 25-6-03 (Page 146)

"… now you do not comprehend this grace, but soon a time will come when you will lament for these messages. That is why, little children, live all of the words which I have given you through this time of grace and renew prayer, until prayer becomes a joy for you. …"

25-8-1997 (Page 121)

"…Today I thank you for living and witnessing my messages with your life. …"

25-6-1999 (page 130)

"… I wish that each of you become a carrier of my messages. I invite you, little children, to live the messages that I have given you over these years. This time is a time of grace. …"

25-2-1996 (Page 113)

"…Today I am happy to see you in such great numbers, that you have responded and have come to live my messages. …"

25-6-1995 (Page 110)

"… I invite you all to have more trust in me and to live my messages more deeply. I am with you and I intercede before God for you but also I wait for your hearts to open up to my messages. …" 25-5-1994 (Page 105)

"… accept my messages as in the first days of the apparitions and only then when you open your hearts and pray will miracles happen. …"

25-9-1993 (Page 102)

"… I invite you to open yourselves to God and in your hearts to live with God, living the good and giving witness to my messages. I love you and wish to protect you from every evil, but you do not desire it. Dear children, I cannot help you if you do not live God's commandments, if you do not live the Mass, if you do not give up sin. I invite you to be apostles of love and goodness. ..."

25-10-1993 (Page 103)

"... if you do not pray and if you are not humble and obedient to the messages which I am giving you, I cannot help you. ..."

25-4-1994 (Page 105)

"... I desire to thank you for living my messages. I bless you all with my motherly blessing and I bring you all before my Son Jesus. ..."

25-6-1998 (Page 125)

"... I am calling you to listen to the messages and then you will be able to live everything which God tells me to convey to you. ..."

25-7-1985 (Page 43)

Križevac 1984.
Meditating at the 4th Station on the Way of theCross

The Purpose and Mysteries of the Holy Rosary

The purpose of the Holy Rosary is to draw people into prayer through the principal events in the history of our salvation, and to thank and praise God for them. There are twenty mysteries reflected upon in the Rosary, and these are divided into the five Joyful Mysteries, the five Luminous Mysteries, the five Sorrowful Mysteries and the five Glorious Mysteries. Blessed Pope John Paul II proposed that these Mysteries be fitted into the weekly cycle of praying the Rosary as follows:

Sunday: The Glorious Mysteries
Monday: The Joyful Mysteries
Tuesday: The Sorrowful Mysteries
Wednesday: The Glorious Mysteries
Thursday: The Luminous Mysteries
Friday: The Sorrowful Mysteries
Saturday: The Joyful Mysteries

The Joyful Mysteries: Monday, Saturday

The Annunciation
The Visitation
The Nativity
The Presentation
The Finding of Jesus in the Temple

The Sorrowful Mysteries: Tuesday, Friday

The Agony in the Garden
The Scourging at the Pillar
The Crowning with Thorns

The Carrying of the Cross
The Crucifixion

**The Luminous Mysteries or
Mysteries of Light: Thursday**
The Baptism in the Jordan
The Wedding at Cana
The Proclamation of the Kingdom
The Transfiguration
The Institution of the Eucharist

The Glorious Mysteries: Sunday, Wednesday
The Resurrection
The Ascension
The Descent of the Holy Spirit
The Assumption
The Coronation

The Recitation of The Holy Rosary

In response to requests on the method of recitation of the Holy Rosary we offer the time honoured custom and practice of praying the Rosary.

One begins by blessing oneself with the cross and saying the Apostles' Creed.

On the first bead, the Our Father is said and on the next three beads three Hail Marys, followed by the Glory be to the Father for the Pope's intentions.

Then follows four groups of five mysteries. Each mystery, or decade, with its own theme for meditation, begins with the Our Father, followed by 10 Hail Marys, concluding with the Glory be to the Father and the Fatima prayer.

"O my Jesus, forgive us our sins, save us from the fires of hell, and lead all souls to Heaven, especially those most in need of Thy mercy."

Finally the 'Hail Holy Queen,' and then the following prayer is recited:

'O God whose only begotten Son by His Life, Death and Resurrection has purchased for us the rewards of eternal salvation, grant we beseech Thee that meditating on these Mysteries of the most Holy Rosary of the Blessed Virgin Mary, we may imitate what they contain and obtain what they promise through the same Christ Our Lord, Amen.'

The Sacrament of Penance and Reconciliation

Preparing

We prepare for it by opening ourselves up, reflecting upon the areas of darkness in our lives into which God so deeply desires to shine a light.

God's love is unconditional. It is not conditioned on my being better, or my overcoming anything, or even my being good at all. God loves me. I am always precious in the eyes of the One who made me and desires to embrace me with the gift of complete freedom, in everlasting life.

Celebrating Reconciliation

Reconciliation is what God does. Receiving it and celebrating it is what we do. For those of us who are Catholics, the Sacrament of Reconciliation is a most natural way to celebrate God's reconciliation. We used to think of this sacrament as only about confession.

One of the great recoveries in our Christian history is to rediscover the meaning of the Sacrament. When we become reconciled with God ,three things remain: to receive it deep within our hearts, to celebrate it, and to participate in the healing process.

In the Sacrament , my personal journey is joined with the mystery of God's saving love, as seen in the scriptures, and in God's desire to save us all. I admit that I am a sinner, express my sorrow, and I name the places in my life where God is shining a Light into what I have done and what I have failed to do. Then God's forgiveness is proclaimed out loud—for me to hear and rejoice in: "May God grant you pardon and fill you with God's peace.

Healing

Part of the Sacrament of Reconciliation is to seek the healing I desire. Often that will simply be prayer. Sometimes, I need to make choices about what I can practice doing, and what I can practice avoiding.

May Our Lord grant us all the gift of Reconciliation.

Excerpt from http://www.creighton.edu/CollaborativeMinistry/reconciliation.html

The Way of the Cross

Station 1 - Jesus is sentenced to death

Station 2 - Jesus takes up His Cross

Station 3 - Jesus falls the first time

Station 4 - Jesus meets His Mother

Station 5 - Simon helps Jesus carry the Cross

Station 6 - Veronica wipes the face of Jesus

Station 7 - Jesus falls the second time

Station 8 - Jesus consoles the women of Jerusalem

Station 9 - Jesus falls the third time

Station 10 - Jesus is stripped of His garments

Station 11 - Jesus is nailed to the Cross

Station 12 - Jesus dies on the Cross

Station 13 - Jesus is taken down from the Cross

Station 14 - Jesus is placed in the Tomb

Holy Places for reflection

In the Church grounds

St. Jame's Church
Adoration Chapel
Confessional Area and St. Leopold's statue
The Dome
Candle Shrine – on the opposite side to
Confessional Area
Statue of Our Lady Queen of Peace
at the front of the Church

Statue of the Risen Christ

Way of the Cross – at this statue
The Holy Rosary – Mysteries of Light

Fr. Slavko Barbaric's Grave – Cemetery

Apparition Hill (Podbrdo)

Blue Cross at Apparition Hill (Podbrdo)

Cross Mountain (Krizevac)

• "... These days, especially, go on the mountain and pray before the Cross."
30-8-1984 (page 30)

• "Pray at the foot of the Cross for peace."
6-9-1984 (page 30)

MAP OF MEDJUGORJE AREA

N W E S — MAP NOT TO SCALE

KRIZEVAC CROSS MT.

MT. PATH

STNS OF CROSS

ROAD

ROAD

PODBRDO/APPARITION HILL

STATUE OF O.L.

ROSARY MT. PATH

BLUE CROSS AREA +

ISNOX/BERG?

ROSARY MT. PATH

CENACALO OASIS OF PEACE

PATH ACROSS FIELDS

MOTHER'S VILLAGE

SCHOOL ROAD

SMALL POST O.

ROUNDABOUT

WATER TAP

P. INFORMATION OFFICE

P. BOOK SHOP •

ADORATION C. •

CONFESSIONALS

CONF. HALL

CEMETERY FR STATUES & GRAVE • STNS. IF CROSS •

RESS. ST

MEDICAL CENTRE

DOME

CANDLE SHRINE •

TOILETS WATER O.T.

STATUE OF OUR LADY

©ELEANOR McFADDEN 231

Basic tips for travelling to Medjugorje - midseason

Listed below are some very basic tips for mid-season in Medjugorje, when the weather can be wet and changeable. Winters are very cold and summers very hot. Dressing in layers solves the problem.

Convertible Mark (KM) is the currency

Euro, dollar and sterling are acceptable

Small bible, rosary beads (may be purchased on arrival)

Camping stool with back (for church)

FM radio, earphones and small sound recorder for talks

Adaptor for round two pin plug (hairdryers, mobile phones etc.)

Torch and extra batteries (for the mountain)

Woollen hat and gloves

Sun block, sunhat and sunglasses

Good flat walking shoes for climbing rocky terrain.

Good raingear and a change of shoes

Haversack, waist bag, umbrella (small)

Hot water bottle if required

Mosquito repellant, alarm clock

Tea bags and biscuits (optional)

Where can this book be obtained

MEDJUGORJE

Paddy Travel (Marian Pilgrimages Office)

Joe Walsh Tours Office, Dubrovnik Restaurant

Ars Sacra, Vestment Shop (shop nearest the Church across the river)

Kathy's Kitchen

Emmanuel Shop

Irish Medjugorje Centre

IRELAND

Veritas Shops -

Dublin (01) 878 8177

Cork (021) 425 1255

Sligo (071) 916 1800

Derry (028) 712 668 88

Letterkenny (074) 912 4814

Monaghan (047) 84077

Mary Mediatrix Shop,
12 Upr. O'Connell St., Dublin
(beside Gresham) (01) 8781085
Derek Farrell (01) 846 2671

Publisher's Note

We wish to thank the parish of Medjugorje, the Irish Centre, Joe Walsh Tours, Marian Pilgrimages,

Paddy Travel, Ars Sacra, Kathy's Kitchen, Ray Donnellan at Medjugorje Herald, Irish outlets at Veritas, Cork, Mary Mediatrix Shop, Dublin, Derek and Ann Farrell, our friends and particular our hostesses in Medjugorje, for the enormous support in promoting the book.

The Messages in this 2015 illustrated Edition have been taken with kind permission, from the Medjugorje Parish Website, as in the earlier seven editions.

Our Lady's Messages were received in Croatian and because of the literal translation may, in some instances, lack fluency for the English speaking reader.

Special thanks are due to Ivanka Leko of Grafotisak, for her unfailing support with this series from the beginning.

We thank you sincerely for your prayers and acknowledge the time and work given to producing this series. We really need your support to keep the book in production each year. In buying a copy for yourself or another, you are in turn helping us to spread the messages and so to fulfil the intentions of Our Lady. Each book you buy helps to defray the costs of producing the series. Publishing costs been what they are, any donation you choose to contribute ensures continued production. Without your help it would be impossible to continue.

"You are the ones responsible for the messages. The source of grace is here, but you, dear children, are the vessels which transport the gifts......give the gifts to others with love, and do not keep them for yourselves." *(Message of 8 -5- 1986 (Page 59)*

Resurrection Statue

Confessional Area

Vicka's house

Bijakovići Blue Cross Area

*Section of vast area for
outdoor Holy Mass*

*Main Street,
Medjugorje*